MARKS
OUT OF
XI

England's Winter Tour of India and Australia
1984–1985

VIC MARKS

GUILD PUBLISHING LONDON

This edition published 1985 by Book Club Associates by arrangement with George Allen and Unwin (Publishers) Ltd.

Set in 11 on 13 point Plantin by Fotographics (Bedford) Ltd, and printed in Great Britain by Mackays of Chatham Ltd

Contents

The author and publishers wish to thank
Adrian Murrell of All-Sport Photographic Ltd
for his assistance in supplying the photographs herein.

1

Waiting for the Telephone Call

O moral Gower, this booke I direkte to thee. *Chaucer*

At the beginning of September county cricketers, no matter how jaded or disillusioned with their profession, cannot avoid speculating upon the deliberations of the selectors of England's touring party. This year I was no exception, for I knew I had a good chance; my colleagues at Somerset had been predicting my inclusion since the middle of August whilst I had remained cagey, but quietly, very quietly confident. I had been fortunate to be chosen for the previous two winter tours (this is not false modesty, look at the statistics) but now for the first time my record in county cricket clearly justified selection.

So on Wednesday 12 September, whilst recovering from an enthralling finale to the season against Nottinghamshire, I was eager to know whether I would be wintering in Devon or Delhi. The answer was provided not by Peter May or Donald Carr or Tony Brown, but as usual by a local journalist – this year Chris Ducker of the *Bristol Evening Post* narrowly pipped Ian Seymour of HTV West. This is the normal method by which English cricketers hear of their selection; against a background of telephones and tapping type-writers someone blurts out 'Congratulations' and you realize you're in. For cricketers no news is usually bad news.

My reaction to it was one of relief rather than jubilation; at least the uncertainty was over and my winter was suddenly beginning to take shape, but there were no spontaneous whoops of delight from the Marks' household, no frenetic dashes to the Tesco wine counter; in fact, there was little elation at all. Chris informed me of the full party, which was:

Gower (captain)	French
Gatting (vice-captain)	Lamb
Allott	Marks
Cowans	Moxon
Cowdrey	Pocock
Downton	Robinson
Edmonds	
Ellison	Brown (manager)
Foster	Gifford (assistant manager)
Fowler	Thomas (physio)

By noon the telephone had started ringing. I had forgotten that the West Country was so well endowed with such an assortment of radio stations and local newspapers – Radio Bristol, Devon Air, Somerset County Gazette, Western Morning News, Western Daily Press . . . I felt compelled to treat my dog to an unscheduled mid-day walk along the River Exe, a far cry from the Ganges, yet suddenly very tranquil.

This provided a brief respite rather than a permanent escape from the journalists. I wanted to avoid them for no obvious reason; they're hardly vipers in the West Country and I hadn't battered my wife recently or flattened Ian Botham in a Taunton pub; nonetheless I carried out the interviews with reluctance. I expressed delight, a modicum of surprise (such humility) and spoke of exciting challenges to come and I expect I praised the perspicacity of the selectors, which seemed a more sensible course than the 'I'm not too fussed, I'd expected to go, why on earth have they left him behind' approach.

I was, however, a little alarmed by my lukewarm response to selection, even though I could explain it. I had been playing cricket continuously since April 1981 and had just about survived a demanding and drought-ridden season with my sanity intact. Along with many other current professionals I think that English cricketers are required to play too much for their own good. By September, if a trophy still beckons, they are desperately delving for the last dregs of inspiration and energy; if out of contention, they don't always bother so that the standard of cricket is reduced and the spectators are sometimes cheated. At the end of the 1984 season we were all surprised to read of several counties disciplining their players for various misdemeanours as some of our more sensitive cricketers began to wilt under the sheer volume of cricket. Let's play less, but to a higher, more competitive standard.

Moreover, after two winters abroad with England I was under no illusions about the pitfalls as well as the pleasures of touring. A winter tour would mean another long separation from my wife and daughter, who bear the major burdens of a cricketer's life. (I stand by that even though she's just left the room.) However, on reflection, I realised that life wasn't really that cruel. I recognised that my enthusiasm would be rekindled by the end of October, that it is the aspiration of every county cricketer to represent his country (either give up or stop moaning) and that I had enjoyed most of my previous tours despite England's recent dire record. And I needed the money. We receive £9500 for the tour of India and another £1500 if we go to Australia plus an additional £200 for every previous tour. From Cornhill Insurance the squad receives £2000 for each Test match victory. This is obviously more than we would hope to earn if we were not selected but it amounts to far less than my non-cricketing friends imagine; for some reason they assume figures of £20,000 plus for the tour. Modern cricketers are often reminded in the columns of the *Daily Telegraph* and elsewhere that financially they are very fortunate to be playing in this era. Reading *Cricket and Empire* by Ric Sissons and Brian Stoddart at least makes this assertion a matter for debate. They revealed that on the 1932/3 tour to Australia the professionals received £400 plus 'merit money', which was allocated by the MCC after the tour; this varied from £175 each for Hammond, Larwood and Sutcliffe to £75 each for poor old Bowes, Mitchell and Tate. In 1933 mineworkers, who admittedly were poorly paid, received just over two pounds per week, whilst a skilled male worker in a large industrial city received between £3 and £3. 10s. A leading pro cricketer in county cricket would receive approximately £10 a week if there was a first class match, £3–4 if not. These figures suggest to me that cricketers' wages have not mushroomed to the extent that many would have us believe.

On hearing the party my mind focused not on its merit, but on the potential companions and the notable absentees. In August, Ian Botham had announced that he was unavailable to tour, a decision which was greeted with almost universal approval. (I gather that Scunthorpe United's reserve centre-half was a little disgruntled, not to mention Darlington's precious centre-forward). Ian had toured every winter since 1977 and needed a break if he was to remain the lynchpin of England's cricket team throughout the eighties. Inevitably, his absence would create an enormous vacuum both on the field and in the team room. We all know that only he can change the course of a Test Match within a session, but who is going to fill our Yorkshire opening batsman's shoes with shaving foam, deafen us with Toyah or lift the depression of colleagues by sheer exuberance? Occasionally he can be utterly infuriating, but he's impossible to dislike and never boring. I shall miss him and so will millions of Indian cricket lovers.

Nevertheless his absence may ease the roles of Gower and Gatting. Ian is such a dominant personality that it is difficult not to be overshadowed by him; at Somerset it has taken the mortals a long time to adjust to playing with the likes of Richards and Botham, to overcome any inferiority complex and not to be over-reliant upon them. Unwittingly his mere presence in the England side might have reduced the authority of the captain and vice-captain; now, at least they will make their decisions more confidently without feeling answerable to him. Even though the parallel is unfair, I suspect that Gower was more assertive in Lahore in March than at Lord's in June, likewise Gatting was a more positive batsman. For the first time Mike will be England's undisputed attacking middle order batsman and I'm sure that this knowledge coupled with the added responsibility of the vice-captaincy will help him to forget his past Test record and to reproduce his Middlesex form for England.

So there may be some compensations in the absence of our leading all-rounder; in the ideal world Gower will return from India as the undisputed boss, Gatting a proven Test batsman and Botham will be rejuvenated – someone had better ring Melbourne to tell the Aussies to stay at home next summer and to concentrate on the America's Cup.

Personally I would have welcomed the inclusion of Tavare and Roebuck as they are two of my favourite dining partners. Chris listens to me; I listen to Pete.

Twice in Championship cricket Chris has deposited my first delivery of the match into the River stand at Taunton much to first slip's amusement. I'm the only person able to induce this and hereby throw down the gauntlet to Mr Heineken. Chris will prefer to erase September 1984 from his memory. Having been recalled by England for the last two Test Matches of the summer (we all assumed in preparation for India and maybe the vice-captaincy) he scored a dour, deadpan 14 in two hours against Sri Lanka when a breezy ten in two overs would have enhanced his tour prospects further. Kent then proceeded to lose the Nat West final by the narrowest of margins and a week later he found himself omitted from the tour party and relieved of the Kent captaincy. His successor has a formidable record to live up to – 7th and 5th in the Championship – and twice Nat West finalists.

Pete was probably further from the selectors' minds despite playing superbly in mid-season when the selectors were casting around for Daniels for the den. He may be one of those cricketers whose temperament and technique are especially suited to Test cricket – we may never know. Anyway I'll regret his absence and so should you as he would have been writing this book.

Other cricketers who should have been clinging to their transistors or telephones on that Wednesday would have included Broad, Randall, Barnett, Miller, Hemmings, Benson and Thomas in decreasing order of expectation.

The party is very inexperienced, with an average age of 27+; only Pocock (38), Edmonds (33) and Lamb (30) are older than I am, so I suppose I've made that dreaded transition from being a promising youngster to a wily old pro – there's nothing in between. Ian Botham has taken more Test wickets than all the bowlers put together and three of the batsmen have yet to play in a Test Match.

An unusually high number of us will be strangers to one another on 30 October. It will be interesting to observe what friendships emerge and how quickly the newcomers adjust to the demands of touring. Half-baked judgements upon our domestic opponents will be rapidly reviewed once we've roomed together for a few weeks. My first room-mate as an England tourist was Robin Jackman and the prospect didn't fill me with glee for Jackman was that obnoxious little medium-pacer whose theatrical histrionics when I missed his outswinger convinced me that he was a completely undesirable character. Within a week I'd changed my mind (his early morning tea was perfectly brewed) and by the end of the tour I considered him a close friend and was lamenting his retirement and the absence of his special brand of abuse at the Oval.

I've toured with only six of the party before. I'll look forward to reuniting with Graeme Fowler, the impish extrovert from Accrington, who ensures that the theories of his mentor, David Lloyd, live on. In Australia in 1982 Lloyd wrote several letters of encouragement to Graeme, who was being bowled by beamers and run out without facing; in one he observed that Jackman, who had not been selected for at least six weeks, had acquired the nickname of Lucan in England because 'since he's left the country, no one has seen or heard of him'.

Whenever his huge reserves of restless energy permit, Graeme sits down and thinks deeply about his game. When he was first selected for England, he believes that he under-performed because he was so conscious of trying to play like an England player, with the right elbow pointed and feet positioned to MCC coaching book standards. Now he plays like Fowler of Lancashire. There's a lesson there for all of us; we should stick to the methods that have brought us success and selection and not alter our game just because we have an England sweater on.

Allan Lamb, one of only four players on this tour to survive all six Test matches this summer (along with Gower, Fowler and Downton), should vie with Gower as the side's leading runscorer with his confidence restored after four Test centuries in England in 1984. We have roomed happily together on previous tours even though my early morning constitution has yet to come to terms with his pre-breakfast routine, which involves switching on the radio and the television simultaneously and at full volume whilst bellowing down the telephone in pursuit of his laundry. Up to now only Botham has managed to check this procedure. Norman Cowans will have an endless supply of reggae music or is it the same record? Neil Foster, I presume, will be as unselfconscious as ever; if his Vichysoisse isn't hot, he'll send it back. Gower and Gatting, as captain and vice-captain, will enjoy the luxuries of a single room.

Unsurprisingly, I applauded the choice of spinners. Pat Pocock, along with John Emburey, has been regarded as one of the best English off-spinners of the last decade; but in these utilitarian times his inability to score any runs has kept him in the wilderness. It is a tonic to watch him bowl because he obviously enjoys himself so much constantly flirting with subtle variations of pace and flight. In his youth (so I'm told) he was often criticised for straining for too much variety at the expense of accuracy but at 38 the impatience of youth should have passed him by, after all he toured with Chris Cowdrey's father. In the past I've learnt from watching him bowl from a distance; hopefully this winter I'll learn a lot more from close quarters.

Phil Edmonds of the high classical action is the left arm spinner; his non-selection over the past few years has mystified the critics. The official line has always been that he has been omitted on purely cricketing grounds, but this has convinced no one. He's obviously an independent soul, reluctant to compromise, occasionally unreliable, but on his day the best left-arm spinner in the country. I suspect that recent tour selections have placed too much emphasis on 'good tourists' – even though I have probably benefited from this policy. The last two tours have been harmonious, but singularly unsuccessful. It must be right to pick the best players whatever threat they may appear to pose to 'team spirit'; a successful side is quickly united, at least on the field, and this has to be the prime consideration.

Of the newcomers I don't know Robinson, French and Moxon at all. The Notts pair clearly earned their selections after consistent performances in the Championship. Moxon has been picked on his potential and a few gnarled old pros (not me, I've only just graduated to 'wily') will consider him very fortunate. Playing for Yorkshire does, however, appear to be an advantage for I notice that Bill Athey's 1800 runs for ailing Gloucester hardly thrust him into the limelight. Chris Cowdrey is the most interesting choice, one of Peter May's hunches (Moxon being the other). In contrast to his father he's a gritty, down to earth cricketer who doesn't look very pretty. His straightforward, positive approach more than atones for any technical deficiencies and I'm sure he will be in the 'good tourist' category. He'll view September 1984 in a slightly different light to Chris Tavare.

On 14 September a large buff envelope from the TCCB containing tour notes and instructions, two contracts and the itinerary, arrived. At the moment my knowledge of India is scant so the fact that we have fixtures at Chandigarh, Faridabad and Gauhati made little impact. A brief sortie to the Tiverton library hasn't helped since the only relevant book on the shelves, 'Plain Tales from the Raj', describes India in pre-Pocock days; however I've vowed to do some more research before I leave. It is too easy for the modern cricket tourist to ignore his surroundings; the itinerary is crowded and the hotels are usually comfortable and alluring, but it would be a shameful waste of an opportunity if we didn't try to discover something of Indian culture and traditions.

The tour notes refer to various administrative details; visa application forms, the required vaccinations, fittings for the team uniform, passport photos and P45's. There are also regulations about advertising on clothing and the writing of press articles; whatever is written here will be scrutinised by the TCCB, but read on anyway. I note with pleasure that the loss of my right arm is insured for £40,000, an increase of £10,000 up on last year, my little toe returns £1200 and my spinning finger £8000; nonetheless the advantages of self-mutilation have so far been rejected.

On 2 October I attended my medical at Bernard Thomas' Edgbaston Health Clinic, where the examinations have been held for the last three years. They have now become more extensive and thorough in an effort to forestall any unnecessary setbacks such as in 1980 when it was discovered after a month in the West Indies that Brian Rose's eyesight was inadequate for Test cricket.

To my surprise the dreaded caliper test decreed that I was only 2–4 lb overweight after three weeks of complete inactivity. The doctor took vast quantities of my blood amongst other things, prodded, poked and pronounced me healthy. As I was leaving he gave me a slip of paper carrying two instructions – 'See your dentist' and 'Get fit'. Dutifully I've arranged to play squash with my dentist; I shall have to lose as we have an appointment on Friday.

2
Delhi

Thursday 1 November

At 9.30 on 31 October, five hours after our arrival in Delhi, Mrs Indira Gandhi was shot by two of her Sikh security guards. As the members of the England touring party meandered down to a mid morning breakfast, jet-lagged and bleary-eyed, the news spread rapidly through the restaurant, bringing instant wakefulness. The press corps was already huddled together in an animated group planning their new responsibilities as their editors vacated the front pages.

Twenty-four hours later everyone is still stunned, nervously awaiting the reaction of the Indian people to the assassination. From our room I can see smoke billowing into the sky as the Hindus vent their anger upon the Sikh population; a Sikh petrol station is alight and a Sikh school. Someone has counted fourteen separate fires in the distance. Rumours abound; of tourists fleeing from the centre of riot-torn Delhi without their luggage, seeking the relative security of our suburban hotel; of two Sikh hotels being burnt to the ground. Outside people are observing the fires from the rooftops of their flats. Yet below us in an unused car park a group of ten year olds are playing cricket; amongst them is one Sikh child. They ape their heroes; the bowler runs and bowls like Kapil Dev and there is an interminable delay between deliveries.

We are instructed by the British High Commission to remain in our hotel. Yesterday a group of British journalists and photographers were attacked – without serious injuries – as they made their way towards the hospital to which Mrs Gandhi was rushed. The Prime Minister, Rajiv Gandhi, has called for calm, which I regard as an ominous sign.

We can only sit and speculate. The atmosphere is unreal; although we are so close to this catastrophe, TV viewers in England are probably better informed about what is happening two miles from here. Around the swimming pool in the luxurious grounds of the hotel bodies are draped across the sun beds, soaking up the sunshine, apparently oblivious to the events of the last 36 hours. But everyone betrays a little nervousness. An elderly gregarious American lady, intent on discovering the charms of India, advocates yoga to members of the England team, demonstrates her fitness by touching her toes and dives into the swimming pool – at the shallow end. She emerges in distress with a gashed forehead and Mike Gatting, chivalrous as ever, shepherds her to safety.

A twelve day mourning period has been declared, during which there can be no competitive cricket. Today's scheduled practice has been cancelled. Our only means of exercising is in the small hotel gymnasium. After a 3000m run on the running machine – it would have been 2500m until Pat Pocock adopted the Sam Mussabini role – I stopped to glance at the *Times of India* and overheard the receptionist's telephone conversation.

'Oh no . . . how could they? . . . why won't the police come? . . . Get in touch with . . . he must do something.'

I don't know what had happened but it was all very disconcerting.

However the hotel is functioning remarkably smoothly as we wander around feeling helpless and exposed, observing the fires and monitoring new ones. The hotel staff silently deliver the omelettes and pots of tea but they do not want to be drawn into conversation about the tragedy, like a couple zealously entertaining their guests whilst their marriage is in turmoil, they are too polite or too embarrassed to unburden themselves to random strangers. So our meals arrive promptly along with a mechanical, preoccupied smile; whatever disasters occur beyond it is important for the staff to keep their coveted jobs in a Taj hotel. There is disbelief that we are so close to such a monumental event (the assassination took place just two miles away) and a little guilt that we're only concerned with our own welfare and future, whilst a whole nation totters and mourns, angry, self-destructing.

But that is our main concern. Will the tour continue after the period of mourning? Are we safe here? Already there has been one suggestion that we will be encouraged to stay because we could be a stabilising influence, a distraction for the Indian public from recent horrors. I doubt that even in India, cricket is that influential and we would not relish the role of heroic peacemakers. We had been mulling around the team room – there was little else to do – debating every imaginable possibility. No doubt if we have arrived 24 hours later the tour would have been cancelled or at least postponed. In fact the Delhi Cricket Association had not expected us to arrive until the following day; to our surprise there had been no vanguard of officials to greet us at the airport and the *Hindustan Times* reported that 'the England cricket team had arrived to the dismay of the Association's officials'. There were enough problems in Delhi, our arrival understandably faded into significance, merely adding an extra unwanted irritation.

The events of the last two days must be especially distressing for our new tourists. No doubt they had rehearsed in their minds the first week on tour, eager for net practice and to represent England. Now there is nothing but uncertainty and the prospect of being a notorious, quiz question – 'who toured India without playing a game?'

In true British tradition, whilst Delhi was burning I played bridge (Downton making a superlative five hearts at 2 a.m. this morning). Our newly-formed bridge school – it originated in the galley of the BA Tristar which brought us here – plays unconventionally, i.e. there are no conventions. Cowdrey and Gatting have formed a formidable partnership. Gatting, of course, is a swift, impulsive player, positive and aggressive in his bidding. Cowdrey is a more subtle gambler, who is quite prepared to double my three diamonds despite having just one diamond in his hand, thereby frightening me into a ridiculous three spades, which he also doubles with five spades in his hand. The opposition is two from Allott, Downton and Marks. Allott and I are straightforward players who rely heavily on telepathy and the occasional nod or wink. Downton is painstakingly slow and hesitant but completely unmoved by the gentle criticisms of his long deliberations; he also tends to make the crucial contracts much to Gatt's exasperation, who, if you really test his patience, will concede the game in order to speed proceedings. By their bridge perhaps we shall know them.

Sunday 4 November

By the evening of Thursday 1 November the players were sufficiently apprehensive about the situation to summon the management to express our concern. We probably told Tony Brown nothing that he didn't already realise; that there seemed little point remaining in Delhi during the period of mourning; we couldn't play any competitive cricket and our presence there was an unnecessary risk. Withdrawing to Sri Lanka had already emerged as the best option. Our departure could be justified on purely cricketing grounds (we needed competitive cricket) with the clear assumption that we would return, though we were all aware that, if necessary, it would be easier to flee for home from Colombo than Delhi. Moreover there were good reasons for wanting to leave Delhi – the death toll in the capital alone had risen from 70 on Wednesday to 500 on Friday evening.

The manager, whilst appreciating our anxiety, stressed that we were in no physical danger, that he was exploring the possibilities of Sri Lanka but that we should go through the correct channels – the Indian Cricket Board – before leaving. Several of us feared that the difficulty in communicating with the Indian board – its secretary was marooned in Indore because of the curfew – plus all the necessary red tape – would prevent a swift exit to Colombo or anywhere else.

Our only excursion from the hotel was to the British High Commission. On Friday morning we went to use their one concrete net, tennis courts and the open spaces for fielding practice. Throughout the ten minute journey the streets were deserted except for armed police patrolling every 200 yards: obviously maintaining the peace around the foreign embassies was a high priority. The morning was a personal disaster as after ten minutes of fielding I misjudged a catch out of the sun (of course) and failed to make any contact with the ball until it landed on my right eye. Awareness of my own ineptitude is as painful as the blow itself.

In the evening I returned to the High Commission along with the rest of the party, with dark glasses and a darker eye, for drinks in the bar. It was a kind invitation considering the sudden pressure they were enduring. Princess Anne, who had been destined to visit Mother Teresa in Calcutta, was already staying there and they were preparing to welcome Mrs Thatcher, and Messrs Kinnock, Owen and Steel early next morning for the funeral of Mrs Gandhi.

We travelled to the High Commission in a minibus. On the way our Indian driver pulled out in front of a truck, ferrying soldiers, much to our consternation. When we gently questioned the merit of this particular manoeuvre, our driver replied mysteriously, 'Ah, but this is India', as if that explained everything. On reflection those words may have to explain a great deal as the tour progresses.

At the bar, as well as diplomats, there were British businessmen and engineers and even an archetypal Aussie, complaining about the beer and asking very loudly of the whereabouts of the Ashes. However, conversation centred mainly around the events of the last three days as we tried to gain a glimmer of understanding of the frictions within India. The majority of India's Sikh population live in the north and the militants' aim is an independent Sikh State. Four months ago the militants had stockpiled arms in the Golden Temple at Amritsar, which had prompted Mrs Gandhi to take the temple by force. Yet Sikhs and Hindus have coexisted peacefully for centuries: 15% of the army are Sikhs and recently Mrs Gandhi had rejected the idea that those Sikhs responsible for her personal safety should be removed because of the increasing tension. Moreover, many Hindu families in the north raise their first born in the Sikh tradition to encourage peaceful integration. Yet now thousands of the Sikh population were fleeing to hastily constructed refugee camps and not even the experienced diplomats could predict the future which strengthened our belief that it would be wise to withdraw for a while.

On Saturday I watched the funeral of Mrs Gandhi on television. For the last four days on TV there had been no detailed analyses of the events of 31 October, simply pictures of Mrs Gandhi lying in state at the Teen Murti House, where her father Nehru lived as PM, and countless mourners paying their last respects; this scene was briefly interrupted by Rajiv Gandhi's broadcast to the nation: 'Indira Gandhi is no more but her soul lives, India lives. India is immortal. The spirit of India is immortal. I know that the nation will recognise its responsibilities.' But how soon would the nation recognise the futility of vengeance? The ceremony, which was incomprehensible to western eyes, had none of the military precision and attention to detail that we associate with British State funerals. As Mrs Gandhi was borne on a hand pulled gun carriage to Shantavan, the sacred site of the cremation, officers of the army were constantly rushing here and there, waving their arms and issuing last minute instructions. The galaxy of overseas representatives, along with bands of sinister, shaded security guards, were herded into a make-shift stand to observe but not to participate.

Finally Mrs Gandhi, her face in full view, was carried onto the pyre by the military chiefs and members of her family and covered with sandalwood. Rajiv Gandhi circled the pyre seven times and then lit it with a glowing sandalwood stick. As the flames grew he stood aside rigid and expressionless as Mrs Gandhi's intimates ascended the platform to pay their last respects. Despite odd moments of apparent confusion the whole ceremony retained a certain mystic dignity as the Indian sun set in the distance.

In the evening the manager raised our spirits by announcing that we would be leaving for Sri Lanka the next day. He was universally congratulated by the players. During the previous 48 hours Tony Brown, Mark Runacre of the British High Commission and the High Commissioner himself had attended several meetings with officials of the Indian Cricket Board and the Indian Government. Their patience, perseverence and diplomacy had been properly rewarded. For Tony Brown the annual wrangles of the Somerset committee room would be seen in a new perspective.

We all skipped merrily back to our rooms to split up our luggage, packing essentials only for Colombo (Pat Pocock left his bat, but took his helmet). Delhi had been extremely claustrophobic. Since our arrival we hadn't even considered the prospect of playing cricket and enthusiasm for the tour had inevitably waned after five days of uncertainty and inactivity. So we gladly left our baggage with the affable Charlie Pinto, our 'courier', wondering when we'd see it again.

Our 'Flight from Delhi' was utterly devoid of melodrama. We were given a lift to Sri Lanka on the President's Tristar. Whilst the president and two of his Ministers occupied the 1st class cabin, the tour party alone took over the economy class section. We sighed with relief; stretched our limbs, sipped sparkling wine, nibbled shrimps and for the first time contemplated playing cricket. I suspect Dunkirk was trickier.

3

Sri Lanka

As we motored towards our hotel in Colombo at 8.30 p.m. we were faced with a sticky dilemma regarding the coach windows. If shut we were drenched in sweat as it was 29°C and humid, if open we were drenched by the rain of a tropical thunderstorm, no satisfactory compromise was reached and the pessimists amongst us envisaged a week in Sri Lanka watching the rain fall.

The prospect of an early night was dented by the presence of the New Zealand cricket team, which was en route to Pakistan. They had just completed two one-day games against Sri Lanka with honours shared, another indication of the growing stature of Sri Lankan cricket. They warned us of the heat and the tendency of the wickets to be moist in the morning, providing movement for the seamers, before flattening out as the sun rose.

I ended up with Martin Crowe and John Wright, the two English based players in the NZ team. Martin asked after his new Somerset colleagues with genuine affection. In 1984, despite being burdened with the tag of Viv Richards' replacement, he quickly won the hearts of the Somerset players and public alike and proved to be another enlightened signing. He's a rare commodity amongst cricketers – a perfectionist and a team man. At Taunton he spent hours coaching and talking with the young uncapped players so that he ended up as something of a father figure to cricketers of his own age. The sages at the county ground reckoned that he compared favourably with Greg Chappell in 1969 and 1970 – high praise indeed.

He had found a season's county cricket an enjoyable and valuable experience marred only by the volume of cricket and the John Player

League. As a perfectionist the Sunday competition was abhorrent to him and he gained no satisfaction from any personal success in it.

John Wright has become less idealistic after ten years continuous cricket. After a few lagers he expressed in his usual articulate and humorous way that he struggles to be properly motivated every day of his cricketing life. He relies upon a pride in his own performance and a healthy patriotism.

The approaching Pakistan Test series did not excite him enormously. He was, however, relishing the challenge of playing against the West Indies in the Caribbean in March – that would be the ultimate test of his ability. I decided that anyone who was eager to face the current West Indies attack was worthy of the highest admiration.

We also discussed what lingers in the back of the minds of all cricketers of my age and beyond – the need to create options for the future. Professional cricket can all too easily become a trap especially with the (additional) lure of a county benefit. There is a danger that cricketers continue to play simply because there is nothing else that they can do. We agreed to swap notes when all the cricketing nations converge upon Melbourne in February.

In the morning I was given a brief introduction to Colombo by an old Oxford colleague, J. D. Wilson. He took me to the new home of the Sri Lankan Government which is situated in the middle of a lake. He assured me that the site was not chosen for security reasons and that there was no immediate danger of a Tamil uprising (after Delhi the whole party had become very security conscious). Colombo was a safer place to live in than London, an assertion which would have settled any man's nerves – twenty years ago.

We practised in the nets for two days in scorching heat. Creaking, groaning muscles reminded everyone that a cricket tour was beginning – we had almost forgotten. Everything was organised by assistant manager Norman Gifford.

Norman, like Robin Jackman, can be an irritating opponent. If a batsman is blocking him and the game is stagnating, he is not averse to informing the batsman of his assessment of the situation. Tim Robinson for instance, whose only confrontation with 'Giff' has been in the middle, was a little uneasy before the tour began about the choice of assistant manager. Any anxiety was quickly dispelled. Norman likes to keep the game moving to the extent that he's renowned for bowling before the batsman has settled. 'If I'm ready then he should be too.' If he's not aggressive and combative then he's unsure whether he's giving 100%. 'If I'm not ticking, I'm not working.'

After twenty-five years as a professional cricketer, he retains a marvellous enthusiasm for the game, which has increased since his move to Warwickshire, he loves being involved; the cricket itself still tickles his competitive instincts and he has countless friends within the game. Despite his age he can relate very easily to modern cricketers, no matter who they are. Characters as varied as Norman Cowans, Allan Lamb, Graeme Fowler and myself can speak to him with confidence about any cricketing problems and his straightforward common sense that has accrued over the decades will provide chinks of light.

Norman's day starts when he gives an early morning call to each room of the touring party. How pampered we must seem as we travel around the world; the manager keeps the passports, picks up the bills for evening meals and laundry, thrusts boarding cards into our hands and Giff wakes us up each morning like a lovable old prep. school matron. If anyone is late for the bus, Norman will impose the appropriate fine – presently £1 a minute; lack of punctuality can cause intense irritation on tour so the fines are severe. At the moment Lamb and Cowans are the most in debt; the burden of captaincy has undoubtedly improved David Gower's timekeeping.

When we arrive at the practice ground, Norman inspects the nets while Bernard Thomas puts us through our stretching exercises. These rarely vary so I regard them as part of the waking up process. Next, fielding practice. The close fielders (Gatting, Lamb, Edmonds, Cowdrey) disappear with the captain, whilst the outfielders dutifully follow Giff to some remote corner of the ground, Norman is the best purveyor of outfield catches I know; he has developed the knack of stretching each fielder to the limit – a full sprint and you can reach them. He quickly gets to know his players. The catches for Pocock and, sad to relate, Marks demand less speed across the turf than those of Fowler and Robinson. All the while he bellows encouragement 'Come on, Percy, this one's a caught and bowled', 'This one to win the match!'.

Then he organises the bowlers and batters for the two nets –invariably two seamers and a spinner. If anyone starts slogging or ambling up to the crease from two paces, Giff has a sharp word to say, but that's not necessary at the start of the tour. Everyone is anxious to find some rhythm after two months rest. Nets are of much greater importance on tour than during the domestic season. At

Somerset, for instance, I cannot recall seeing Peter Denning or Brian Rose having a net after 10 May unless they are returning from injury. I only feel obliged to have one after an embarrassingly long run of failures. We have so many chances to bat in the middle in England that, for some, net practice is inessential. On tour, the opportunities are far more limited and net practice becomes the only means of 'regaining one's touch'. As the tour progresses, greater powers of self discipline will be required to ensure that net practice is fruitful and beneficial.

As the bowlers tire and the lower middle order batsmen come to the crease, the attack is augmented by Norman and Tony Brown. The manager's arm has dropped a little since his Gloucestershire days but the ball still swings and lands in the right place; he quietly relishes any dismissal. Over the last two winters Norman must have bowled 2000 overs in the nets; I've faced a fair proportion of these and can recall receiving three half-volleys outside the off stump: the habits of a lifetime die hard. By the end of the session his shirt is drenched, he reaches for his pipe and ribs some member of the team, usually Allan Lamb, about the day's effort.

He is always ready to talk cricket yet he spends little time actually coaching unless we ask for specific advice: he recognises that we've all reached our present status despite or because of various technical idiosyncrasies: it is too late to attempt massive overhauls, but he tries to instill confidence in those who lack it – 'Remember they're as terrified as you, even Gavaskar. Put the pressure on them!'

One three-day game and a one-day game were swiftly organised. The selection commitee (Gower, Gatting, Gifford and Brown) omitted Moxon (ill), Cowdrey and Allott (groin strains), French and Marks (fit) to play against the President's XI. I recognise that it is ridiculous to place too much emphasis upon the first selection, but I am conscious of being the third spinner in the party. I have a reputation of being a one-day specialist (which the statistics justify), and lacking the penetration necessary in longer games. Certainly Edmonds and Pocock extract more bounce off the wicket which increases the chances of those bat/pad catches reaching the close fielder. I am also aware of the possibility of not playing Test matches in India and being enlisted just for the one-day internationals.

My publisher, who I hope is sufficiently removed from England's cricket management to be fallible, ascribed to these jottings the working title of 'View from the Balcony' – and I still signed his contract. The best way for me to ensure a Test place is to score some runs.

Richard Ellison will long remember his first day playing cricket for England abroad as he spent fifty minutes stuck in the hotel's lift thereby missing his much coveted breakfast. Richard, an intelligent man (he's a qualified teacher), manages to disguise this fact easily because of his slow, deliberate speech. During the first fortnight away he was very subdued, perhaps unsure of his surroundings and new colleagues, yet when he recounted his thoughts and experiences in the lift in the team room in those deep, solemn tones, everyone was reduced to fits of uncontrollable laughter. Our compassionate assistant manager chose not to fine him as he scrambled into the team bus.

The senior players dominated England's efforts against a young, talented Sri Lanka side. Maybe they were better equipped to adjust to competitive cricket after all the uncertainty of the previous week. Our runs were scored by Gower, Gatting and Lamb, the side's three most experienced batsmen. The Fleet Street corps simply had to dust up the usual epithets – Gower, stylish, graceful; Gatting butchered in his Middlesex persona and Lamb was supremely confident, if a little subdued by his standards. Our spinners were the most successful bowlers and exercised the greatest control, though no one managed to tame another Sri Lankan, de Silva, who, aged 18, scored an exhilarating century after being struck on the head by Neil Foster. The match was deemed to be a satisfactory start, even though both opening batsmen failed. As the *Daily Telegraph* correspondent remarked, England need Fowler/Robinson opening partnerships, not Heath Robinson.

The one-day game against a full strength Sri Lankan side was halted after 38 overs when rain of monsoon proportions flooded the ground: within three-quarters of an hour the dressing rooms were also awash. During the 2½ hours of play the Sri Lankans batted with flair and maturity to reach 178 for 5. Phil Edmonds developed a nervous stutter in his run up which resulted in him delivering the ball from a standing position: he was feeling unwell so hopefully that was the cause. My bowling was patchy; I tended to overpitch and never gained sufficient confidence to introduce any variations. My nine overs cost 47 runs and several pressmen commented afterwards that they had seldom seen me punished so severely in a one-day international. These remarks actually raised my spirits and my confidence. With reluctance I should also add that I dropped a straightforward catch at long on; my colleagues, supportive as ever, congratulated me on getting my hands to the ball and avoiding any further facial damage.

On the last two tours a Social Committee, comprising three members of the party, has been formed to provide entertainment at various stages during the trip. In Australia Miller, Jackman and Botham appointed themselves; last year in NZ and Pakistan Bob Willis appointed Marks, Fowler and Foster; this year to my astonishment Marks and Fowler have been reappointed along with Chris Cowdrey. This year our efforts will be centred around Christmas, but there will also be functions whenever boredom threatens. Naturally these functions sometimes require finance and the Social Committee is entitled to impose fines upon the members of the party for various misdemeanours. In Colombo we held our first fines meeting. Most of the fines are neither worthy nor suitable for repetition: nonetheless here are a few harmless examples.

Edmonds, who is doing a lot of work for LBC radio and *The Mail on Sunday*, was fined for staying at our hotel instead of the Taj with all the other pressmen.

Pocock was fined for his constant references to cricketers that only Gifford and Brown had ever heard of.

Lamb fined for being inconsiderate to his room mate, Edmonds, by demanding to sleep with the curtains closed. Henry needs little sleep and likes to watch the sun rise.

Brown is not exempt. After bowling a succession of half-volleys in the nets at Colombo he summoned the groundsman and a tape measure, assuring us that the pitch was too short. The pitch was of perfect length.

Gatt for being fat.

For some obscure reason we are known as 'The Mafia'.

The unscheduled visit to Sri Lanka was an undoubted success. Our hosts were eager to please and organised everything we needed – except a drop in temperature. The practice had been valuable and more importantly our expedition had begun to resemble a normal cricket tour. Everyone, from the manager downwards, was more relaxed and on our last evening we enjoyed some of the pleasures of 'the paradise island'. A few contrived to attend the US marines annual ball; no doubt thirty years ago we would have all packed our dinner jackets but the British ability to improvise was soon in evidence.

However our stay ended on a sad note. Martyn Moxon, who had spent most of the week in bed with a 'Delhi belly', learnt that his father was ill. A flight home was immediately arranged by the manager. The next day his father died, before Martyn could arrive.

BOARD PRESIDENT'S XI v ENGLAND XI

Played at C.C.C. Ground, Colombo. November 7, 8, 9
Toss: PRESIDENT'S XI Match Drawn

BOARD PRESIDENT'S XI

D. M. Vonhagt	c Downton b Cowans	6	c Fowler b Edmonds	53
C. P. Amerasinghe	c Robinson b Foster	7	c Gower b Pocock	27
S. Warnakulasuriya	c Downton b Ellison	5	c Edmonds b Pocock	0
P. A. De Silva	c Cowans b Pocock	105	c Lamb b Ellison	13
*R. S. Madugalle	st Downton b Edmonds	46	(7) c sub (C. S. Cowdrey) b Edmonds	12
A. Ranatunga	c Lamb b Pocock	42	(8) not out	10
R. S. Mahanama	not out	37	(5) b Pocock	8
†R. G. De Alwis	c Foster b Cowans	42	(6) c Ellison b Pocock	1
R. J. Ratnayake	c Gatting b Cowans	4	not out	10
E. A. R. De Silva	c Downton b Foster	2		
G. N. De Silva	did not bat			
Extras	(LB2)	2		
Total	(9 wkts dec)	298	(7 wkts)	134

Fall of Wickets:
1st Innings: 1–14, 2–14, 3–33, 4–132, 5–191, 6–221, 7–285, 8–291, 9–298.
2nd Innings: 1–49, 2–49, 3–70, 4–85, 5–99, 6–114, 7–119.
Bowling:
1st Innings: Cowans 15–3–59–3; Foster 15.3–6–37–2; Ellison 11–1–45–1; Edmonds 33–10–93–1; Pocock 19–6–62–2.
2nd Innings: Cowans 9–6–31–0; Foster 7–1–25–0; Pocock 19–5–57–4; Ellison 7–2–12–1; Edmonds 6–3–9–2.

ENGLAND XI

G. Fowler	c Madugalle b G. N. De Silva	1
R. T. Robinson	lbw b Ratnayake	2
M. W. Gatting	c Vonhagt b E. A. R. De Silva	97
*D. I. Gower	c Ranatunga b G. N. De Silva	86
A. J. Lamb	c Warnakulasuriya b Ratnayake	53
R. M. Ellison	run out	14
P. H. Edmonds	c Amerasinghe b E. A. R. De Silva	2
†P. R. Downton	b E. A. R. De Silva	0
N. A. Foster	not out	7
P. I. Pocock	c De Alwis b G. N. De Silva	5
N. G. Cowans	did not bat	
Extras	(LB3 NB3)	6
Total	(9 wkts dec)	273

Fall of Wickets: 1–2, 2–17, 3–183, 4–192, 5–230, 6–255, 7–259, 8–261, 9–273.
Bowling: G. N. De Silva 22.3–5–77–3; Ratnayake 22–5–70–2; Ranatunga 10–0–45–0; E. A. R. De Silva 29–9–60–3; Warnakulasuriya 2–0–10–0.
Umpires: A. C. Felsingel and E. C. Seneviratne

SRI LANKA v ENGLAND

Played at P. Saravanamuttu Stadium, Colombo. November 10
Toss: ENGLAND Match Drawn

SRI LANKA

S. Wettimuny	b Gatting	43
†D. S. B. P. Kuruppu	b Edmonds	24
R. S. Madugalle	c Gower b Gatting	25
R. L. Dias	c Robinson b Foster	45
A. Ranatunga	c Lamb b Foster	36
*L. R. D. Mendis	not out	0
P. A. De Silva		
A. L. F. Demel		
D. S. De Silva	did not bat	
J. R. Ratnayeke		
V. B. John		
Extras	(LB4 NB1)	5
Total	(5 wkts, 38 Overs)	178

Fall of Wickets: 1–52, 2–90, 3–104, 4–178, 5–178.
Bowling: Allott 5–1–15–0; Foster 6–0–25–2; Edmonds 7–0–39–1; Ellison 6–0–29–0; Marks 9–0–47–0; Gatting 5–1–19–2.

ENGLAND

G. Fowler, R. T. Robinson, M. W. Gatting, *D. I. Gower, A. J. Lamb, R. M. Ellison, V. J. Marks, P. H. Edmonds, †B. N. French, N. A. Foster, P. J. W. Allott.
Umpires: F. R. S. De Mel and P. W. Vidanagamage.

4

Jaipur, Ahmedabad, Rajkot

Amidst the neat political graffiti and the vivid cinema posters, which are surely more dramatic than the films themselves, one sign stood out as we travelled towards the Taj Mahal Hotel in Bombay after a three hour flight from Colombo.

'Keep your alms from extended palms. Don't encourage able beggars.'

Along with Graeme Fowler I made my first unofficial excursion into India from the team's hotel. We headed for the nearby Gateway of India but within 30 seconds of leaving our air-conditioned haven we were overwhelmed with offers of hashish, marijuana, cocaine and women. Readers of the *Mail on Sunday* may be surprised to learn that we rejected all of them. After inspecting the Gateway, which housed an odd mixture of tourists and gawking, prostrate Indians, we wandered along the promenade gazing at the dozens of tankers loitering in the bay. Foxy has become an ardent photography enthusiast and has some sophisticated equipment so I acted as his lens wallah. Finally we turned into a smaller back street where an eight year old, cherubic Indian girl caught his photographic eye. The lens wallah was summoned and he started clicking. Within seconds we were surrounded by the girl, her brother and sister and mother begging for rupees. They pursued us for the quarter mile back to the Taj, gently clutching our arms, persistent and pathetic. We only possessed Sri Lankan rupees and we finally persuaded another English-speaking hawker to explain that we had no Indian money and we withdrew to the peace of our hotel. But the dilemma remains: Should we scatter some rupees amongst the destitute or 'discourage able beggars'?

From Bombay we flew to Jaipur, the capital of Rajasthan – 'the Abode of Kings'. Apart from unusually stringent security checks there was no obvious evidence of a simmering volcano within India and the fears for our safety, so fervent in Delhi, rapidly evaporated. In the newspapers a return to normality was reported along with frequent analyses and portraits of Mrs Gandhi and soon the announcement of the general election dominated the news pages. Indian newspapers, including the tabloids, are far more politically orientated than their counterparts in England. There must be great scope for Rupert Murdoch in India, though I wouldn't wish him upon the Indians.

On a batsman's paradise, Gower inserted the President's XI, presumably on the basis that the wicket would not deteriorate and that it might assist the fast bowlers in the first session. Indeed, Norman Cowans took two wickets in the morning. He does not always inspire confidence. Norman's opening overs are often wayward and expensive yet he picks up wickets and this knack will probably ensure him a Test place.

Phil Edmonds however was our best bowler, even though he lost his run-up again. In the nets there is no problem; in the middle he stutters up to the wicket like a duck on a river bank contemplating the advantages of a swim. It is not unknown for spinners to lose their run-up. Norman Gifford has experienced the stutters and just occasionally I've forgotten on which foot I start. If I reach that point and I have to think hard which it is then the situation is hopeless. In fact I couldn't tell you now which foot it is; in normal circumstances I just set off and all is well at least until the ball is released. The remarkable thing about Henri's stutter is not that he's suddenly acquired it, but that it has a negligible effect upon his bowling. His perfect action and strong left arm enable him to retain his control.

As I entered the ground on the second day, the players in front of me suddenly halted to stare towards the wicket. Has the pitch been mutilated by Sikh activists? Has a herd of cows meandered onto the square? No, Bishen Bedi was bowling in the nets to the youngsters of the President's XI. Bedi, a test selector, is more portly now, but as he ambled up to the wicket in shorts and training shoes, he still displayed the effortless classical action, the loop and the ability to gain bounce from the wicket. I'm always mesmerised by his pre-delivery routine as he flicks the ball from hand to hand as if it is an extension of his body. Later in the tour we learnt that he had decided to make a comeback in the Ranji trophy.

Henri asked Bishen's advice about his run-up problems but there was no immediate improvement. I remarked that his approach had become purely decorative anyway: he had bowled superbly the day before off two paces: surely if the bowler had no idea when the ball would be finally released the batsman was less likely to achieve any sort of rhythm. The stutter might be a positive advantage but Henri declared that aesthetically the process was unsatisfactory. Both left-arm spinners agreed upon the benefit of running straight up to the stumps. Therefore the ball is required to spin less to find the edge of the bat or gain an lbw decision.

At Jaipur any lbw appeal might be upheld by Swarup Kishan, India's answer to Dickie Bird, their senior umpire, who is instantly recognised by his bulk, his massive floppy hat and betel-nut-stained teeth. At this stage of the tour everyone is conscious of endearing themselves to the umpires and the bowlers, in particular Paul Allott, who toured India in 1981/2, enjoyed some friendly banter with him – 'stand further back please Swarup or else collision'. Over the years Swarup has developed a vaguely comprehensible form of broken English which is interspersed with the odd, incongruous English swear word. Goodness knows who taught him those.

We scored plenty of runs. Tim Robinson was solid and assured, a little reminiscent of Graham Gooch in one of his less belligerent moods. Gower in carefree mood launched an onslaught on the spinners with a series of lofted drives and on the third morning Richard Ellison and I shared a century partnership against a wilting bowling attack. I succumbed carelessly, caught at deep mid-wicket. On dismissal I wasn't too perturbed; I had timed the ball well and felt in control but fifteen minutes later I chided myself for lack of application and greediness. It is a luxury to bat in such favourable conditions and at the beginning of a tour foolish not to make the most of them. The match ended as a sedate draw enlivened only by Chris Cowdrey's first wicket for England. Chris has been nicknamed 'Prince' because of his aristocratic demeanour and the fact that a groin strain prevented him from bowling for a fortnight. So he would wander over to the nets with his pads on, have a knock, graciously thank the bowlers and then leisurely return to the dressing room for some light refreshment.

For two nights we had stayed in an innocuous functional hotel on the outskirts of Jaipur. On the second evening we attended a function given by the governor of Rajhasthan and on our way back the bus was halted at the Rambagh Palace Hotel, a former maharajah's residence of awesome size and splendour. Tony Brown promptly summoned the hotel manager, asked whether he had room for twenty Englishmen and booked us in for the two remaining nights. Previous tour managers in my experience would not have reacted as swiftly but the move was characteristic of Tony's style; forthright, instinctive and prepared to act on the spur of the moment. His decision was rewarded when he inherited a suite which was large enough to provide two indoor nets and we all enjoyed the spacious luxury and the resident snake charmers and folk dancers of the Rambagh Palace even if we were aware that our stay there would constitute something of a honeymoon period.

On the rest day we rode elephants up to the Amber fort, seven miles to the north of Jaipur and then visited the famous Palace of the Winds – the pink palace in the centre of Old Jaipur. The journey in hired cars was hair-raising – even for me. There appears to be no highway code in India, just a vague expectation that you proceed on the left hand side of the road unless you are a cow. The road was crammed with an endless stream of cyclists, carts drawn by hands, bullocks and camels, three-wheeled taxis and a few cars whose horns are regarded as a far more essential piece of equipment than the brakes. As we dutifully took our photos of the pink palace we were immediately surrounded by beggars, some lepers, some with mutilated limbs, all helpless. For those of us new to India the experience was shattering even though we had been warned what to expect. At Ahmedabad it was worse.

As we motored towards our hotel in the dry state of Gujarat Foxy wondered aloud, 'It's 8.30 on a Friday night, what am I doing in Ahmedabad'. We responded that Ahmedabad couldn't be that different from Accrington and that he and Paul Allott in particular should feel at home as the guide books describe it as the 'Manchester of India, the industrial city of the NW'. There was, however, little prospect of rain.

We witnessed more squalor on the way to the ground. Amidst the shacks there were two dead donkeys and a prostrate camel, hogs rummaged amongst the litter. Huge drainage pipes skirted the road and Charlie Pinto told me that they were rented as homes – for 50 rupees a month until they are laid in the ground. I asked him whether anyone ever escapes from these hovels and he replied, optimistically, 'Just a few'. Solkar, the Indian test player of the 70's whom you may remember (though not so vividly as Geoff Boycott), was one. We also noticed an increased presence of armed police; we had an escort to the ground and half an hour before the start the stadium held more policemen than spectators.

It is a fine new arena, constructed in just nine months after its architects had spent a summer selecting the best aspects of English test centres, but the Englishmen in November still felt far from home. For three days we performed abysmally on a slow, easy paced wicket unlike the inaugural match at the stadium against the West Indies when the wicket disintegrated. We were dismissed for 216 in 60 overs as the batsmen established themselves at the crease and then threw their wickets away through carelessness and complacency. Of the runscorers Gatting was the victim of a laughable run-out decision and I was totally deceived by a slower ball. This is a feature of Indian medium pacers, because the wickets are generally unresponsive they are more adept at variation of pace. In England wickets are taken by seamers because of movement off the wicket, here the deception often has to be achieved before the ball bounces. Earlier Graeme Fowler had been similarly undone and was caught and bowled. He observed that a massive adjustment was necessary after the series against the West Indies; last summer, whenever a full length ball emerged it was a rare run scoring opportunity not to be missed. In India you have to be prepared to miss a few of these opportunities.

We were equally self destructive in the field as we dropped three straightforward catches and the Indian U25's gave their elders a lesson in patience and the art of building an innings. Worse was to follow on the third day as we succumbed through inept batting abetted by some strange umpiring to be dismissed for 113. Sivaramakrishnan, an 18 year old leg spinner, and Sharma, a tiny off-spinner, took four wickets each. The first cricketing crisis of the tour had arrived. In one match all the frailties of the touring party had been exposed – lack of penetration in the bowling and fickle batting.

Of our two tormentors, I was more impressed by Siva. He looks even younger than his eighteen years and I was surprised to learn that he had already toured the West Indies with India. Odd as it may seem, I have only played against three 'professional' leg spinners – Intikhab, Abdul Qadir and Robin Hobbs. Siva differs from all these in that he is small, frail and teetotal and though at present he may lack the accuracy of Intikhab or the deceptive loop of Qadir, at Ahmedabad he mesmerised us as we struggled to read the subtleties of his variations.

The dressing room was hushed at the end of the game; we were shocked by the ineptitude of our performance. Gower broke the silence, though there was little he could say: we knew we had played terribly, but it was not the end of the world, better now than in the first test. Don't get depressed, but learn from the experience, think about the match and there would be a team meeting to discuss our cricket at Rajkot.

At the meeting the discussion concentrated upon our batting even though batting failures are far more difficult to analyse than errors in the field. Gower stressed the importance of acquiring a large total in the first innings and that we should think in terms of batting for two days. Unnecessary risks should be eliminated and once set, batsmen should maintain their concentration. This might be helped by the batsmen constantly encouraging one another and noticing when their partner was beginning to play too loosely. Patience, as the captain had stressed at Lord's in October, was the key to a successful tour of India – whether at airport lounges, official functions or at the crease. All good sense, if familiar.

Henri broadened the discussion by talking about our overall attitude to playing cricket abroad. We should not forget that we were representing England and that millions were charting our progress, or lack of it, back home. It was all too easy to become distracted from the cricket by so many new experiences in India. The coach journeys to the ground with the squalor, the dead donkeys and camels and the gawkers resulted in our minds being far from the particular cricket match in progress. We should be aware of this problem and consciously try to counteract it. Henri was most impressive and is the most intriguing character on the tour. At times remote and aloof, at others helpful and perceptive and always aggressive on the field. The social committee have already fined him for not being the troublemaker that he's alleged to be as he has been conspicuously co-operative with the management and he has earned the gratitude of everyone by procuring some high quality scotch from Johnnie Walker. Yet occasionally he's prone to deafness and is absent from team meetings and photographs: eventually he emerges wide-eyed and mystified asking quietly why no one informed him of the meeting. His studied innocence always provokes suspicion.

Whatever the quality of the meeting, something clicked against the West Zone. On a featherbed wicket we compiled 456 for 3 with contrasting centuries from Fowler, Robinson and Gatting whereupon Gower was forced to declare as Vengsarkar started bowling lobs, which were totally meaningless as practice. Our bowlers fared little better: again Henri, still stuttering, was comfortably our most menacing bowler and he is emerging as the lynch pin of our attack. Vengsarkar, India's number three, scored a double century, initially uncertain but soon aloof and dominant. My own performance was utterly unproductive especially as I suspected that the eleven at Rajkot was selected as a potential test team. I took no wickets in 40 overs and even though I could point to a couple of dubious rejections of bat/pad and lbw appeals, the same nagging problem of a lack of penetration haunted me. After long wicketless spells I often fall into one of two traps: either my bowling becomes mechanical and devoid of any expectation of a wicket or in desperation I seek too much variety in the vain hope that I'll produce the unplayable ball. Nor did I enhance my chances by failing to score in our meaningless second innings. Batting in a dead game poses special problems of motivation to all cricketers, but in the past Test places have been secured in such situations.

Rajkot is something of a backwater with a population of a mere 350,000. They rarely see touring sides so the match excited the locals. Before the start we were introduced to the mayor whilst members of the local brass band hammered out Colonel Bogey with enormous gusto though completely independently. As usual we were garlanded by the prettiest hotel receptionist and one evening we were entertained by the local folk dancers. Fowler, a frustrated pop star, and Cowans, betraying his West Indian origins, both accompanied the musicians on the drums and the language barrier was thereby overcome. An eminent palmist (apparently he had predicted Mrs Gandhi's death) foretold success and prosperity for several of the tourists between the ages of 27 and 36, but could not commit himself about the forthcoming test series.

The hotel was the most spartan that we have encountered. We slept in shirts and pants (only Tavare and Ellison have packed pyjamas over the last three years) in a vain attempt to avoid mosquito bites. Our washing facilities consisted of one big plastic bucket and one small plastic bucket and the pillows were like lumps of granite. Fowler gloated as he had followed the advice of Chris Tavare and is carrying his own pillow around India. In Rajkot he could have sold it to our sleepless assistant manager at a vast profit.

No doubt the tourists of thirty years ago would have relished such luxury, but I can report there were few serious complaints. Our tolerance threshold may be somewhat lower by February.

The evenings inevitably dragged – one was passed with an epic snooker/table tennis contest between the press and the players: both sides claimed victory. The social committee held its second meeting: this time we compelled our members to participate: after nearly four weeks together any inhibitions were gradually disappearing and everyone was prepared to make fools of themselves, if necessary. There were a few undemanding charades, for example Martyn Moxon gave us 'Life in the Fast Lane', Phil Edmonds 'Tales from a Long Room' and David Gower 'Heroes and Contemporaries', all guessed within seconds.

Surprisingly five days in Rajkot were now preferable to being in Sri Lanka: the papers reported 130 Sri Lankan soldiers killed in the north following a Tamil uprising; there was now a curfew in Colombo. As we packed our bags we congratulated ourselves upon finally managing to avoid an international crisis.

BOARD PRESIDENT'S XI v ENGLAND XI

Played at S.M.S. Stadium, Jaipur. November 13, 14, 15
Toss: ENGLAND XI Match Drawn

BOARD PRESIDENT'S XI

*A. D. Gaekwad	c Gower b Ellison	23		
P. Shastri	c Gatting b Cowans	6	(1) c Edmonds b Cowdrey	30
M. Azharliddin	b Cowans	2	not out	52
A. Malhotra	not out	102		
Gursharan Singh	b Edmonds	41	(4) st French b Edmonds	0
S. Mudkavi	c Cowdrey b Edmonds	15	(5) not out	21
†K. S. More	not out	4	(2) c French b Cowans	12
A. Patel				
A. R. Bhat	did not bat			
R. R. Kulkarni				
Randhir Singh				
Extras	(W5)	5	(B1 LB1)	2
Total	(5 wkts dec)	198	(3 wkts)	117

Fall of Wickets:
1st Innings: 1–18, 2–20, 3–44, 4–127, 5–165.
2nd Innings: 1–24, 2–69, 3–70.

Bowling:
1st Innings: Cowans 13–4–29–2; Allott 12.1–4–33–0; Ellison 14–3–42–1; Edmonds 30–9–48–2; Marks 15–3–41–0; Gatting 1–0–5–0.
2nd Innings: Allott 9–1–29–0; Cowans 6–1–35–1; Cowdrey 4–1–6–1; Edmonds 11–5–15–1; Marks 9–1–30–0.

ENGLAND XI

G. Fowler	c More b Bhat	28
R. T. Robinson	c and b Mudkavi	81
M. W. Gatting	c Mudkavi b Bhat	36
*D. I. Gower	c Shastri b Kulkarni	82
C. S. Cowdrey	b Kulkarni	8
R. M. Ellison	not out	83
V. J. Marks	c Azharliddin b Mudkavi	66
P. H. Edmonds	c Kulkarni b Patel	6
†B. N. French	b Mudkavi	19
P. J. W. Allott	not out	5
N. G. Cowans	did not bat	
Extras	(B5 LB15 W4 NB6)	30
Total	(8 wkts dec)	444

Fall of Wickets: 1–56, 2–142, 3–221, 4–244, 5–279, 6–394, 7–404, 8–436.
Bowling: Kulkarni 22–2–78–2; Randhir 18–2–72–0; Bhat 31–4–97–2; Patel 30–3–112–1; Mudkavi 18–2–65–3.
Umpires: P. D. Reporter and Swarup Krishan.

INDIA UNDER-25 XI v ENGLAND XI

Played at Gujarat Stadium, Ahmedabad. November 17, 18, 19
Toss: ENGLAND XI   INDIA UNDER-25 XI won by an innings and 59 runs

ENGLAND XI

G. Fowler	c and b Prabhakar	19	lbw b Ghai	9
R. T. Robinson	c Sivaramakrishnan b Ghai	11	c Viswanath b Sharma	3
M. W. Gatting	run out	52	b Prabhakar	16
A. J. Lamb	c Shastri b Prabhakar	18	c Sivaramakrishnan b Sharma	34
*D. I. Gower	c and b Shastri	21	c sub (S. Mudkavi) b Sivaramakrishnan	8
R. M. Ellison	c Shastri b Sivaramakrishnan	5	b Sivaramakrishnan	3
V. J. Marks	b Ghai	37	st Viswanath b Sivaramakrishnan	2
†P. R. Downton	b Sharma	11	st Viswanath b Sivaramakrishnan	6
N. A. Foster	b Ghai	11	not out	20
P. J. W. Allott	c Madhavan b Ghai	14	c Viswanath b Sharma	10
P. I. Pocock	not out	2	c Ghai b Sharma	0
Extras	(B4 LB4 W1 NB6)	15	(B1 LB2 NB3)	6
Total		216		117

Fall of Wickets:
1st Innings: 1–36, 2–40, 3–62, 4–105, 5–117, 6–145, 7–183, 8–198, 9–209, 10–216.
2nd Innings: 1–12, 2–17, 3–65, 4–71, 5–75, 6–79, 7–85, 8–86, 9–115, 10–117.

Bowling:
1st Innings: Ghai 12.5–2–42–4; Prabhakar 10–2–48–2; Sharma 12–2–41–1; Kanwilkar 3–0–15–0; Sivaramakrishnan 10–1–38–1; Shastri 11–1–29–1.
2nd Innings: Ghai 10–1–36–1; Prabhakar 9–3–21–1; Sivaramakrishnan 20–11–27–4; Sharma 12–6–22–4; Shastri 8–3–8–0.

INDIA UNDER-25 XI

†S. Viswanath	c Downton b Allott	31
K. Srikkanth	b Pocock	92
M. Azharuddin	c Lamb b Marks	151
Gursharan Singh	lbw b Allott	0
R. Madhavan	not out	103
R. Kanwilkar	c Ellison b Pocock	1
M. Prabhakar	run out	0
R. S. Ghai	not out	0
*R. Shastri		
L. Sivaramakrishnan	did not bat	
G. Sharma		
Extras	(B1 LB9 W2 NB2)	14
Total	(6 wkts dec)	392

Fall of Wickets: 1–65, 2–141, 3–145, 4–385, 5–388, 6–388.
Bowling: Allott 27–4–99–2; Foster 22–5–59–0; Ellison 34–10–86–0; Pocock 22.2–2–94–2; Marks 10–3–34–1; Gatting 5–0–10–0.
Umpires: S. K. Bose and D. R. Dotiwalla.

WEST ZONE v ENGLAND XI

Played at Racecourse Ground, Rajkot. November 21, 22, 23, 24
Toss: ENGLAND XI Match Drawn

ENGLAND XI

G. Fowler	c Jadeja b Patel	116	(5) b Patel	2
R. T. Robinson	b Sandhu	103	(6) not out	34
*D. I. Gower	st Pandit b Gudge	57		
M. W. Gatting	not out	136		
A. J. Lamb	not out	30	(8) st Pandit b Patel	22
P. H. Edmonds			(1) c Sandhu b Keshwala	8
R. M. Ellison			(2) c Sandhu b Patel	25
V. J. Marks	did not bat		(3) b Keshwala	0
†P. R. Downton			(4) c and b Patel	35
N. G. Cowans			(7) c Gudge b Patel	10
P. J. W. Allott				
Extras	(B2 LB8 W1 NB5)	16	(B1 LB1)	2
Total	(3 wkts dec)	458	(7 wkts)	138

Fall of Wickets:
1st Innings: 1–190, 2–246, 3–317.
2nd Innings: 1–33, 2–33, 3–46, 4–48, 5–99, 6–111, 7–138.
Bowling:
1st Innings: Kulkarni 22–5–58–0; Sandhu 31–7–99–1; Keshwala 5–0–12–0; Patel 39–7–102–1; Gudge 26–6–114–1; Rajput 4–1–10–0; Patil 6–0–35–0; Vengsarkar 1–0–7–0; Jadeja 1–0–11–0.
2nd Innings: Kulkarni 8–1–25–0; Sandhu 6.2–1–25–0; Keshwala 8.4–5–11–2; Patel 18.5–8–42–5; Gudge 10–0–33–0.

WEST ZONE

L. S. Rajput	b Edmonds	79
S. Kalyani	lbw b Cowans	9
*D. B. Vengsarkar	not out	200
S. M. Patil	c Gower b Edmonds	4
B. Jadeja	c Downton b Ellison	48
†C. S. Pandit	run out	22
S. Keshwala	c Gower b Edmonds	19
B. S. Sandhu	c Downton b Edmonds	0
A. Patel	not out	9
R. R. Kulkarni	did not bat	
S. C. Gudge		
Extras	(LB3)	3
Total	(7 wkts dec)	393

Fall of Wickets: 1–20, 2–155, 3–159, 4–266, 5–340, 6–374, 7–374.
Bowling: Allott 14–2–48–0; Cowans 19–4–76–1; Ellison 12–5–28–1; Edmonds 49–18–99–4; Marks 39.2–5–120–0; Gatting 5–0–19–0.
Umpires: B. Ganguli and M. G. Subramaniam.

5

Bombay, First Test

The name Percy Norris meant nothing to us when we returned to Bombay on 25 November; forty-eight hours later he dominated the thoughts of each member of the touring party.

Percy Norris was the British Deputy High Commissioner in Bombay and at 8 a.m. on 27 November he was assassinated on his way to work half a mile from the Wankhede Stadium, the venue for the first Test match.

The news was all the more distressing as we had attended a drinks party at his flat twelve hours before his death. It had been our most enjoyable function of the tour; there was none of the stuffiness and pomposity that sometimes accompany such occasions. Mr and Mrs Norris were genuine cricket enthusiasts; they knew each of the touring party from Gower to French by name and they were perfect hosts, mingling, introducing but never imposing. They had assembled a motley collection of British ex-patriots and several prominent Indians; including former Test cricketers, Vijay Merchant and Dilip Sardesai, both of whom expressed an overwhelming desire that this Test series should provide results; cricketers invariably adopt a more cavalier approach to the game after retirement. Our welcome had been so overwhelming that we lingered long enough to test the patience of our coach driver.

We departed in high spirits yet the next day the tour was catapulted back to the atmosphere of Delhi. We knew something was afoot when we assembled for a team photograph at 9 a.m. The management were huddled together in stunned conversation and when Henri was late (ill informed again) the Manager had to strain to keep his temper. A team meeting was announced for 9.45 a.m. to confirm our suspicions of a new crisis (another change in the itinerary, perhaps) but no one had anticipated such a bombshell.

Practice was postponed: we should stay in the hotel and await further instructions; the Manager would be in regular contact with the British High Commission in Bombay and Delhi. For two hours we assembled in various rooms, speculating about the future of the tour and searching for the World Service wavelength. At first the implications for us seemed more serious than the assassination of Mrs Gandhi; after all Percy Norris was British – so were we. We inevitably linked the two assassinations; might this be an anti-British Hindu backlash since the British had refused to deport the London based Sikh activist, the self-styled President of the Republic of Khalistan, Dr Jaggit Singh Chauhan. Maybe the assassins had chosen Percy Norris in Bombay because our foremost diplomat in Delhi was too well protected. Again there were doubts about our own safety and visions of the tour being cancelled. Indeed the bulk of the English pressmen advocated the cancellation of the tour because of the accumulation of troubles – the assassinations, the continuing uncertainty of the itinerary and the forthcoming elections, with all the potential problems that they might provoke. I had a bet with Scyld Berry of *The Observer* that the tour would continue and the Test match would start as scheduled on the following day. I'm not sure how much I wanted to win it.

At 11.30 a.m. Gower toured the rooms with Gatting (maybe he felt the need of a henchman) to announce that we would be practising within the hour. At the time this decision astonished us; cricket seemed so insignificant in the wake of such a tragedy. Britain's top man in Bombay had just been shot, there were rumours, denied by Tony Brown, that the British community were advised to stay indoors, and we were going off to smack some cricket balls around the outfield of the Wankhede Stadium. In retrospect the decision has gained merit; practising partially distracted our minds from the assassination and halted further wild speculation and there was a Test match scheduled for the next day. At the ground Sunil Gavaskar came to our dressing room and quietly expressed his condolences.

When we returned armed guards had emerged on the third floor of our hotel and from now on we were accompanied by special branch officers on coach journeys, armed with sten guns.

By 6 p.m. when we assembled for our team meeting, we realised that, contrary to the expectations of the morning, the Test match would probably go ahead. The captain, whilst recognising our anxieties, encouraged us to forget what had happened and to concentrate on the cricket. Mrs Norris had sent a message wishing us luck and expressing how much they had enjoyed their last evening together. We marvelled at her bravery.

Gower read out the selected twelve: Fowler, Robinson, Gatting, Gower, Lamb, Cowdrey, Ellison, Downton, Edmonds, Pocock, Cowans and Allott, who was omitted the next day. Obviously there had been a rethink since Rajkot. My analysis was this: two factors dominated the selectors' minds:

(1) It was imperative not to lose the first Test, especially after England's experiences on the 1981 tour when the first Test match proved decisive.
(2) The Bombay wicket was expected to favour the spinners on the last two days; therefore they decided to play Pat Pocock, rather than myself, since we needed our most penetrating spin bowlers. His inclusion would weaken the batting, hence the selection of Chris Cowdrey, who would also have to operate as third seamer.

However, the selection for the first three matches meant that Cowdrey and, to a lesser extent, Ellison were playing after insufficient preparation. Ellison had not bowled with a new ball on tour and Chris Cowdrey had played just one innings of eight back at Jaipur, where he had also bowled five overs: the selectors were asking a lot of a Test match debutant.

The content of team meetings vary according to the captain. Under Willis we would usually analyse the strengths and weaknesses of every opposition batsman in some detail, even though there is just one place to bowl to most batsmen – on a good length at off stump – adjustments to the field placing being far more important. There are a few exceptions. For example in Australia after Kepler Wessells had scored his maiden Test century at Brisbane, we realised that if we bowled at his legs, he got into a terrible tangle and thereafter he was relatively unsuccessful. We would discuss which of the opposition batsmen hooked and whether it was worth feeding him a few bouncers. The more inexperienced batsmen would be enlightened by the senior players about the various attributes of the opposition bowlers.

At Somerset we hardly ever hold formal team meetings: sometimes before one-day finals at Lord's we have a team dinner but our discussion rarely bears any relation to what happens the next day. However they are usually grand social occasions. Last year at Swansea before our first Benson and Hedges zonal match our team talk consisted of 'Let's get stuck in. Back up and watch the sandy bits.' Needless to say, we won the game.

In Bombay Gower preferred not to dwell upon the technicalities too long, but stressed the importance of being in the right frame of mind. It was crucial to want to win and for players and non-players to support each other for six days. A Test match was a pressurised event, draining chunks of our lives and we needed to concentrate at all times, but if we performed to our ability all would be well. He was quite impressive, if a little self-conscious. It does not come naturally to him to deliver Eddie Barlow style 'up and at 'ems', so his observations were reasoned and controlled. His remarks were reiterated in more belligerent style by Mike Gatting.

The first day of the Bombay Test may prove to be the decisive day of the series so it warrants detailed description. It began on a note of black humour. Graham Morris, one of three British photographers on tour, decided to test the efficiency of the officials at the gate. Wearing a jacket crammed with hardware (cameras, in fact) he asked a gateman in his best Irish accent 'Excuse me, I'm from the I.R.A., could you direct me towards the English dressing room, please?' The official politely obliged.

Before the match began two minutes silence, which lasted twenty seconds, was observed to mark the deaths of Mrs Gandhi, Y. B. Chavan, a former deputy prime minister, and Percy Norris and both sides wore black arm-bands. I hope this does not become a regular feature of the tour.

Gower won the toss and unhesitatingly chose to bat. As Kapil Dev and Chetan Sharma opened the bowling for India, I was surprised to note that the stands were little more than half full. On an easy paced wicket with low bounce, there were few alarms. Robinson scored his first Test run with a single wide of mid on and Fowler opened with a four to third man. Gavaskar quickly switched his bowlers, trying Shastri's left arm spinners and Amarnath's gentle away swingers. After ninety minutes we were 46–0 and I nodded to Norman Gifford, with whom I've watched numerous overseas Test matches, that this was an excellent toss to win. Now Gavaskar turned to Siva, the baby-faced leg spinner, who had embarrassed us at Ahmedabad. The previous evening we had not discussed him at length, not regarding him as a serious threat and certainly not rating him in the Abdul Qadir class. This was his second Test match, having played against the West Indies the previous year, and he was obviously nervous, still searching for his first Test wicket. Within ten minutes he had two, both fortuitous.

His fourth ball was a high full toss. Fowler, unsure whether to hit it over mid wicket or down the ground, succeeded only in driving it straight back to the bowler – without bouncing, 46–1. Graeme Fowler was obviously disappointed by his dismissal, but unusually it was tinged with relief. Before the match began, it had occurred to him that if there were any anti British crackpots in the stands, he would be the prime target as England's opening batsman. These fears had not lingered with him during his innings but back in the pavilion they returned. In retrospect such reservations may appear ludicrous but twenty-four hours after an assassination they were completely understandable. In his second over he bowled an innocuous googly outside leg stump; Tim Robinson swept and was adjudged caught behind; he departed slowly shaking his head: 51–2 and Siva was starting to enjoy himself.

After lunch Gatting and Gower proceeded cautiously but without obvious difficulty until Gatting was deceived by Siva's trajectory and was caught and bowled, from a checked drive, 78–3. In Kapil Dev's next over Gower played on: he may have been outwitted. Since lunch Kapil had been attacking David's leg stump with five men on the legside – long leg, square leg, mid on, leg slip and short leg. Early in his innings David has a tendency to hit the ball in the air on the legside and in Australia in 1982/3 he was dismissed several times in this way. On this occasion he refrained from playing any attacking shots in that arc, but when Kapil eventually bowled a good length ball wide of the off stump, David tried to hit it through the sparse off side field. The ball ricocheted onto his stumps, 78–4.

Chris Cowdrey was still buckling his pads when he heard the roar that greeted Gower's dismissal; whilst spared the torturous wait before his first Test innings, he was nevertheless plunged into a situation of extreme crisis as he passed England's captain, anxious to discover who was going to bowl him his first ball in Test cricket. At the other end Allan Lamb hit his first two balls from Siva to the boundary, but quickly clipped a legside half volley from Kapil Dev to Shastri at mid-on, 93–5. In Siva's next over Ellison was bamboozled by a perfect googly, 94–6.

Cowdrey, who is renowned as a doughty fighter in tense situations, survived with Paul Downton until the drinks interval. As I was pouring out the staminade, I suggested for want of anything better to say that these two Kent public schoolboys, one from Tonbridge, the other Sevenoaks, should imagine that they were playing arch rivals Kings Canterbury. Such subtle motivation had no obvious effect as Cowdrey was soon caught by Kirmani from the bowling of off-spinner Yadav, 114–7.

Complete disaster was averted by an eighth wicket partnership of 61 between Paul Downton and Phil Edmonds. Whilst Paul concentrated on defence, Henri lofted Yadav into the stand at long on and then drove his first ball from Siva into the sightscreen. Gavaskar, anxious that his trump card should retain his confidence, immediately withdrew Siva from the attack, much to the relief of English spectators – and Henri. A sharp catch by Gaekwad in the gully ended the Middlesex resistance and at the close of play England had struggled to 190–8. Already everyone was aware that it would require a momentous effort to save this Test match.

The second day's play was frenetic, compulsive viewing and totally unlike what we've come to expect of Indian Test matches. Gavaskar chose not to take the new ball and this decision was soon justified when Siva took the last two wickets giving him figures of 31.4–10–64–6. After 4 overs India were 33–0. Gavaskar began by hitting Ellison on the up past mid-off and then both openers punished a wayward Cowans. Norman can be so infuriating; his first two overs lacked pace and direction, simply because he wasn't loose. Admittedly he had just batted and there was little time to unpad, put on his bowling boots and go outside to bowl a few balls at Bruce French; but in the future he will have to make time. His next four overs were extremely hostile – as quick as I've seen him bowl in Test cricket. He brushed Gaekwad's nose with a vicious lifter and soon after took his first wicket when Gavaskar sparred indeterminately outside the off stump, 47–1. At 59, Gaekwad, lean and bespectacled, reminiscent of Zaheer Abbas in appearance, was stranded in the middle of the wicket after a misunderstanding with Vengsarkar, confirming the view that the morning's play bore more relation to the John Player League than a traditional (5 day) Test match.

After lunch the mayhem continued as Gower persisted with his pace bowlers. Vengsarkar hit four fours from Cowans' first over and the 100 came up in 18.4 overs, of which 84 runs were boundaries. The Indians, reputedly such placid, patient cricketers, were launching themselves at the ball at every opportunity: Vengsarkar tried once too often and was caught at second slip. Sandip Patil's innings, as befits a part time film actor was a dramatic one. Cowans hit him on the helmet whereupon he retaliated by smashing Pocock for two aerial boundaries. However it ended tamely, caught at silly point off Edmonds, who in the excitement had overcome his run-up problems. With Amarnath falling at the same score, 156, England were briefly back in the game, with two new batsmen, Shastri and Kapil Dev, at the crease.

Shastri's reputation entitled us to believe that we would finally see some good old-fashioned Test match blocking, but even he was dancing down the wicket to the spinners, which suggested that the Indians had consciously decided upon a policy of all-out attack. As the partnership began to prosper after tea, Gower summoned Cowdrey to bowl. 5000 miles away in the centre of London, Colin Cowdrey was so stunned by this decision that he proceeded the wrong way down a one-way street, car radio at full volume. A policeman stopped him and began to reprimand him. During the conversation a deafening roar emanated from the car radio heralding Chris' first test wicket, Kapil Dev. Chris Cowdrey was delighted, Colin Cowdrey was delighted and most importantly so was the policeman who ignored the offence. No wonder the British Bobby is held in such high esteem. The 'Prince', who naturally approves of two-over spells, bowled one more over and was withdrawn from the attack. Cowans was recalled and Kirmani, despite several moments of uncertainty, survived with Shastri to the close of play with the score at 286–6.

At the rest day press conference, David Gower refused to connect England's poor performance on the first day to Percy Norris' assassination. Obviously his death had affected our preparations, but it would have been unwise to use the tragedy as an excuse, particularly since several of the British press had been remarkably sympathetic in their columns, referring to 'The Test Match that should never have been played'.

Whilst most of the players involved in the match spent a restful day around the hotel, I played golf with two of our journalists at the Willingdon Club. It's a delightful course, situated in the centre of the city and it is remarkable to find 50 acres of serene grassland amidst the delapidated flats and bustling streets of Bombay. One of my opponents, whilst eulogising about the standard of the greens, rather undiplomatically mentioned that he was hoping for another game on Monday, the fifth day of the Test match.

The third day was more sedate. Gower switched his bowlers around, attacked, defended but all to no avail as Shastri and Kirmani amassed a partnership of 235, a record for India's seventh wicket. Kirmani deflected and square cut and occasionally skipped down the wicket to the spinners whilst Shastri batted with massive assurance, scoring predominantly on the legside. At the age of 22 he conducts himself like a seasoned campaigner on a cricket field: already he's scored 1300 Test runs and he began life as a left arm spinner! As a bowler his greatest assets are his accuracy and ability to gain bounce, rather than vicious spin and subtle variations: at the crease he plays within his limitations – a rich man's David Graveney.

After tea even the eternal optimist Pat Pocock was a little surprised to find himself on a hat-trick as the two Indian centurions holed out to deep midwicket off consecutive balls in response to Gavaskar's demand for quick runs. Soon after the innings was closed leaving England the dreaded fifty minutes batting.

In the third over Tim Robinson was given out lbw to Kapil Dev. He departed even more slowly than in the first innings being convinced that he hit the ball. In the evening he shaved off his embryonic moustache presumably on the grounds that the umpires didn't like the sight of it very much.

Two portly gentlemen dominated the fourth day's play, Mike Gatting and Swarup Kishan. Throughout the morning session, Gatting and Fowler coped with the varied Indian attack with sufficient composure to raise our hopes of saving the game. Even our golfing enthusiast in the pressbox must have been impressed. After lunch Fowler was becalmed against the spinners; a confident lbw appeal was rejected by umpire Ganguli and Siva was close to tears. Gavaskar trotted over from extra cover, put a paternal arm around his shoulder and consoled him. In the next over a far less convincing shout was upheld and it was difficult to avoid the conclusion that the umpire was atoning for his previous decision.

On his return Foxy was furious. Whilst recognising that he had entered a difficult phase in his innings, he had felt confident of batting all day. He had been batting to a strict pattern, which was more defensive than usual playing the spinners off the back foot and relying solely on deflections square of the wicket for his runs.

Gatting now watched with a mixture of disbelief and frustration as England's middle order batsmen came and went; Gower caught at silly point off Shastri, Lamb stumped off Siva and Cowdrey caught at silly point off Yadav. Of the first five dismissals we reckoned that one was legitimate (television replays indicating that Lamb's foot was in the air when Kirmani removed the bails). I know it's very boring for English cricket followers to read, yet again, of criticisms of overseas umpires but Swarup's performance was deemed, at best, incompetent.

Meanwhile, Gatting remained undeterred by Siva, Yadav, Shastri or Swarup. As wickets fell he became more aggressive. When he reached the nineties, everyone was aware of that peculiar torment that afflicts batsmen in pursuit of a maiden century. However he remained outwardly unruffled and without delay achieved the landmark, which surely heralds the turning point in his test career. He finally succumbed on 136 out of 219 runs scored whilst he was at the wicket, caught at long off. Maybe frustration at the earlier umpiring decisions caused this aberration, anyway there was good reason for him to attack the bowling as the English innings was beginning to disintegrate. His departure signalled the end of any realistic hopes of saving the game, despite stern resistance from Downton and Pocock on the fifth morning.

Defending 48, Edmonds and Cowans opened the bowling and caused a few flutters in the Indian dressing room. Gaekwad, comprehensively beaten in the air and off the wicket, was stumped, whilst one of a succession of short pitched deliveries from Cowans was cut viciously by Gavaskar to Gower in the gulley. However Vengsarkar and Amarnath quickly guided India to their first victory in 31 tests.

Even though defeat had been imminent for 18 hours, the final blow was utterly deflating; like the death of an ageing grandparent, the loss is expected and predictable, but the actual moment still hurts.

In the evening we gathered in the team room and the captain reflected briefly on the Test match. Some of the players were still enraged by the umpiring decisions. Gower stated that there would be no official comment to the press, but that he would be informing the Indian board in the conventional manner, i.e. the umpires reports, of his opinion of their performance; there was no easy solution to the umpiring problem; we should try not to worry about them: the game was difficult enough without having to alter our techniques of batting to accommodate the whims of the umpire. He told us that he was confident that we would retrieve the series, we should stick together, work hard and aim to win the second Test at Delhi. Finally the XII for the one-day international at Poona was announced with Marks, the one-day specialist, back in the squad.

In the evening we attended a drinks party hosted by Grindlays, our bankers. Norman Gifford, fortified by a few generous scotches, expressed the view that Siva, who had ended the match with figures of 12–181, would not survive the series. We also speculated about the nature of the next four test pitches, mindful of what happened on Keith Fletcher's tour in 1981/2 when four dreary draws on feather-bed wickets followed the decisive First Test. At his press conference Gavaskar had emphasised the need for more results in Indian Test matches, particularly in view of the reduced crowds. We hope that this is more than shrewd public relations work.

The function was held in the magnificent Crystal Room of the Taj Mahal. It is a majestic hotel, built in the 1880's, which has enchanted onlookers and guests alike, but unfortunately not its architect, who was so distressed when he learnt that it had been built facing the wrong direction that he threw himself fatally from the top floor. David Gower's men, though a little dejected after the First Test, had not yet reached that pitch of despair.

A few days later I had a brief chat with Sunil Gavaskar, an ex-Somerset colleague, about the First Test. I asked him whether the aggression displayed by the Indian batsmen had been premeditated. The answer was no. He never gave instructions to his batsmen on how to play, not wanting to add to their pressures. The rapid run rate would be attributed to (1) wayward English bowling; (2) the vast increase in one-day cricket had affected the nature of Indian batsmanship; (3) after eleven recent tests against the West Indies it was such a relief to face bowling of ordinary proportions that the batsmen couldn't restrain themselves. I mentioned Shastri's aggressive intentions against the spinners and he said that this was now his normal method in domestic cricket.

Sunil also expressed surprise at David Gower's pre-match statements in the press – that England was primarily concerned not to lose the First Test. Psychologically he believed that this had two effects. It put the English batsmen in a hesitant and defensive frame of mind and conversely it gave the Indian team, without a victory in thirty tests, a significant confidence boost. Perhaps we were too concerned with our own frailties to even consider theirs.

INDIA v ENGLAND (FIRST TEST MATCH)

Played at Wankhede Stadium, Bombay. November 28, 29
December 1, 2, 3
Toss: ENGLAND INDIA won by 8 wickets

ENGLAND

G. Fowler	c and b Sivaramakrishnan	28	lbw b Sivaramakrishnan	55
R. T. Robinson	c Kirmani b Sivaramakrishnan	22	lbw by Kapil Dev	1
M. W. Gatting	c and b Sivaramakrishnan	15	c Patil b Sivaramakrishnan	136
*D. I. Gower	b Kapil Dev	13	c Vengsarkar b Shastri	2
A. J. Lamb	c Shastri b Kapil Dev	9	c Kirmani b Sivaramakrishnan	1
C. S. Cowdrey	c Kirmani b Yadav	13	c Vengsarkar b Yadav	14
R. M. Ellison	b Sivaramakrishnan	1	(8) c Vengsarkar b Yadav	0
†P. R. Downton	not out	37	(7) lbw b Sivaramakrishnan	62
P. H. Edmonds	c Gaekwad b Shastri	48	c Kapil Dev b Sivaramakrishnan	8
P. I. Pocock	c Kirmani b Sivaramakrishnan	8	not out	22
N. G. Cowans	c Shastri b Sivaramakrishnan	0	c Vengsarkar b Sivaramakrishnan	0
Extras	(B1)	1	(B4 LB8 NB4)	16
Total		195		317

Fall of Wickets:
1st Innings: 1–46, 2–51, 3–78, 4–78, 5–93, 6–94, 7–114, 8–175, 9–193, 10–195.
2nd Innings: 1–3, 2–138, 3–145, 4–152, 5–199, 6–222, 7–208, 8–255, 9–317, 10–317.

Bowling:
1st Innings: Kapil Dev 22–8–44–2; Sharma 11–4–28–0; Shastri 17–8–23–1; Amarnath 3–2–1–0; Sivaramakrishnan 31.2–10–64–6; Yadav 12–2–34–1.
2nd Innings: Kapil Dev 21–8–34–1; Sharma 9–2–39–0; Sivaramakrishnan 46–10–117–6; Yadav 29–9–64–2; Shastri 29–8–50–1; Gaekwad 1–0–1–0.

INDIA

*S. M. Gavaskar	c Downton b Cowans	27	c Gower b Cowans	5
A. D. Gaekwad	run out	24	st Downton b Edmonds	1
D. B. Vengsarkar	c Lamb b Cowans	34	not out	21
M. Amarnath	c Cowdrey b Pocock	49	not out	22
S. M. Patil	c Gower b Edmonds	20		
R. J. Shastri	c Lamb b Pocock	142		
Kapil Dev	b Cowdrey	42		
†S. M. H. Kirmani	c Lamb b Pocock	102		
C. Sharma	not out	5		
N. S. Yadav	not out	7		
L. Sivaramakrishnan	did not bat			
Extras	(B4 LB2 NB7)	13	(B2)	2
Total	(8 wkts dec)	465	(2 wkts)	51

Fall of Wickets:
1st Innings: 1–47, 2–59, 3–116, 4–156, 5–156, 6–218, 7–453, 8–453.
2nd Innings: 1–5, 2–7.

Bowling:
1st Innings: Ellison 18–3–85–0; Cowans 28–6–109–2; Edmonds 53–6–82–1; Pocock 46–10–133–3; Cowdrey 5–0–30–1; Gatting 7–0–20–0.
2nd Innings: Edmonds 8–3–21–1; Cowans 5–2–18–1; Pocock 2.1–0–10–0.

Umpires: B. Ganguli and Swarup Krishan.

6
Poona – Bombay

Our man in Poona was Mike Gatting, effortlessly scoring his third century in four knocks in the first one-day international. It was an innings of enormous significance for the entire party. After defeat at Bombay, it was vital to win at Poona to restore sagging morale and raise our confidence for the forthcoming tests.

Gatting remained calm and assured throughout the two crisis points of the English innings 47–3 and 130–6, situations in which he has triumphed countless times for Middlesex but seldom for England. So far he has emerged as the most reliable and dominant batsman in the party and the Fleet Street journalists are wracking their brains to explain the transformation; so am I even though I note (with a certain smugness) that I predicted a successful tour for him before we left.

Indeed, around the bars of county grounds throughout the country, one of the main topics of conversation, along with the latest episode of bloodletting at Yorkshire, has been the career of Mike Gatting. For the last four years, he has been the most effective English batsman in county cricket. My present room-mate Chris Cowdrey related Kent's tactics against him – 'In 1981 we tried to bounce him out; in 1982 we tried to spin him out; in 1983 we tried to frustrate him and in 1984 we prayed'.

I have also found him an especially daunting opponent; at Bath in 1984, he responded to his latest omission from the England side with a murderous 258. At the beginning of his innings he prefers to score off the back foot with cuts and pulls square of the wicket. Against the off spinner his backlift almost tickles his right ear and he often dummies to come down the wicket in the hope that the bowler will drop short. Once established, these threats are fulfilled and he pummels the ball to long on or beyond. At the crease he is brimful of confidence, almost arrogance.

At Bath last year, he looked as if he was going to smash every ball I bowled to the sightscreen and by the end of his innings, he did. Whenever he elected to defend one of my off spinners, it was not through necessity but because of some whim as if saying, 'I probably could have hit that ball for six but I'm not a complete slogger, so I've decided to block it as I'll be hitting another to the boundary within the next five minutes'. Fortunately for my ego, he's butchered every spinner in county cricket, even Derek Underwood, the ultimate test.

Yet recent Test bowlers have been much less exasperated by his presence in the England side and everyone has been mystified by his modest Test record (1141 runs at an average of 24.34 before the tour began).

Certainly, in the past he has been hampered by being juggled up and down the batting order. On his last tour to India, he batted at number seven on several occasions, hardly conducive to inspiring confidence in one of county cricket's premier batsmen (though Derek Randall has managed to adjust to this indignity). The technicians can point to a certain fallibility in his footwork against extreme pace – his front foot is sometimes lodged in front of middle and off and he is prone to being lbw playing around his left pad. Yet these explanations are insufficient; he meets Test class opposition in county cricket and prospers.

At Middlesex he is the lynchpin of the batting line up, a position that automatically instils confidence, even though he has never appeared to lack it. In the past in the England team he has often been over-shadowed by the likes of Ian Botham both in cricketing terms and within the social structure of the group and I feel that this has had an effect on his performances out of all proportion. To be confident and to succeed he needs to be the undisputed trump card in the pack and until now, when he is batting at No. 3 and vice-captain, this position has eluded him. Maybe previously he has been torn between the straightforward butchery of his Middlesex days and his notions of the requirements of an England player. When the ball that he would normally hammer to the cover boundary arrived, his instincts would begin the demolition exercise, but then, he would suddenly remember, 'This is a test match, my place is in jeopardy', hesitate and possibly nick it tamely to the keeper. Now there is no sign of any indecision.

As vice-captain on this tour, he provides an excellent foil to the captain. His uncomplicated, bulldog attitude contrasting with the more introspective approach of David Gower. He is our sergeant major, cajoling and badgering the troops in loud, high-pitched tones whilst our captain observes quietly from a distance.

His demeanour on the field fairly reflects his character, straightforward, combative and bustling with energy. He's an avid games player, whether bridge, snooker or golf; he likes to win and usually does, relying upon his native Cockney wit and sharp competitive instincts. Decisions regarding the constituents of his evening meal, a 5 iron or a 6 iron, or whether to take the new ball, are reached swiftly and with complete confidence. At Poona, he allowed himself a few moments respite after his century; but soon he was out of his chair, packing his bags and saying 'Come on let's get back to the Taj to celebrate properly'.

We had travelled the 120 miles from Bombay, most of which appeared to be uphill, by coach. Our five-hour journey was interrupted by a half-hour stop at 'The Stud', a Wild West style restaurant, where the waiters sported jeans, sombreros and moustaches and we devoured baked beans and coffee. I suppose there may also be Indian restaurants in South Dakota, but it was something of a surprise to hit upon this establishment 60 miles east of Bombay.

The match caused great excitment in Poona. Three thousand spectators emerged to watch us practise and afterwards we were officially welcomed by the mayor in a chaotic ceremony at the ground. As the two sides sat down in front of the main stand, the mayor plus any other available dignitaries delivered long, incomprehensible speeches in Hindi. No one seemed to listen; photographers and autograph hunters enveloped us, the jostling and animated conversations continued and our resolute speaker, undeterred, kept speaking. At intervals Henri and Foxy leapt to their feet, clapping vigorously in an attempt to terminate proceedings but to no avail. It was the first time that we've experienced such enthusiasm and mayhem, though Norman Gifford informed us that these scenes accompanied the 1972/3 tourists wherever they went.

The following day, the stadium was packed to its 40,000 capacity. Since their World Cup victory, Indian cricket fans have become obsessed with one-day cricket at the expense of five-day Tests, even though the Indian side had lost its previous nine matches. The wicket, unlike the outfield, was true and Gower, having omitted

Cowdrey, won the toss and chose to field on the grounds that any assistance for the bowlers would be restricted to the first hour of play.

The one-day internationals in India are scheduled to be 50 overs per side but they rarely are. The first innings, which commences at 9.30, closes at 1 p.m. however many over have been bowled and the length of the second innings is adjusted accordingly. At Poona, we bowled only 45 overs, despite using two spinners, an indication of the different pace of Indian cricket matches; the two drinks intervals alone usurp fifteen minutes playing time: in England on Sunday afternoons we can muster 40 overs in 2¼ hours. It is a system which is open to abuse by the captain fielding first, though our slow over rate was not premeditated.

Neil Foster had spent the previous fortnight recovering from a back ailment and then kicking his heels during the Bombay Test. He is a confident, ambitious man, who – quite properly – is frustrated by long periods of inactivity, watching from the sidelines. His first ball clipped the inside of Gavaskar's bat and hit the off stump and all the frustrations of the last two weeks immediately evaporated.

Srikkanth, one of six changes from the Test side, restored the Indian innings along with Vengsarkar yet we always maintained a measure of control.

Recognising the docility of the wicket, we employed deep set fields forfeiting singles but preventing many boundaries and we restricted them to 213 which was deemed satisfactory as we tucked into our corned beef and baked beans (again) at lunchtime. Just before the close of the Indian innings, David Gower became a victim of the treacherous outfield. A straightforward drive to mid on hit him on the nose and caused a deep cut in his nose and he was forced to leave the field bleeding profusely. This mishap resulted in a reshuffle of the English batting order with Marks being promoted to number five – number five for England – if only they printed scorecards in India to decorate the mantelpiece in my living room.

So at 47–3 I joined Mike Gatting and we added 68 together with remarkably few alarms. The dearth of slips in one-day cricket is a definite bonus for me as early in my innings the projected cover drive scutters down to third man with amazing regularity. As the years go by, I have developed a casual saunter down the wicket intended to inform the uninitiated that the shot was intentional. Thereafter, I played rather well and was relaxed enough to rib the Indian captain about his fielding at short mid wicket. At Somerset in 1980, he was nicknamed 'Swoop' because of his stark refusal to dive under any circumstances. Yet here he was in Poona hurling his 37 year old frame over the treacherous outfield like a prep school Norman Wisdom. We were coasting comfortably when I misjudged a run to short fine leg and was eighteen inches adrift at the wicketkeeper's end. Two more wickets fell quickly but Paul Downton batting with much commonsense stayed with his county captain and they guided us safely towards our target.

However, our first victory on Indian soil was delayed for seventeen minutes when a few of the crowd, presumably frustrated by India's imminent defeat, hurled bottles onto the outfield. I can inform readers of *The Sun* that the headlines 'England in Riot Terror – Bottle Barrage Fury' overstated any danger to the English contingent. The incident was inconvenient and frustrating but a mere trifle in comparison to the earlier events of the tour.

Hopefully this victory would mark an upturn in our fortunes, the dawn of a new era, which all tourists must believe in, when they are trailing in a Test series. It certainly made our return to Bombay more palatable along with another stop at 'The Stud'. In the back of the coach, away from the Walkman cassette machines that nowadays accompany most international cricketers everywhere, there was plenty of lighthearted banter at the expense of Gower and Lamb, 'The Thunderbats', who have so far failed to reach double figures in three innings against India. Allan complained of the heat whilst we were batting in the afternoon – 'Why? Had the air-conditioning broken down in the dressing room? Would he be cabling Slazenger for some more batting gloves?'

However, our concern about the form of our two leading batsmen was more serious after the zonal match at Bombay. In our only innings of the match against N. Zone, both failed again though for different reasons. Allan Lamb appeared to be in complete command, disdainfully driving left arm spinner Maninder Singh over the sightscreen. However soon after, attempting to repeat the shot he smashed the ball straight to mid off. Over-confidence had caused his downfall. In the summer of 1984, the West Indian bowling attack had sharpened his concentration, demanding complete alertness if he was to defend his wicket as well as his good looks. Here the threat is concealed, the pitches and the pace of the bowling are inviting in comparison and he has been lulled into being overambitious at the start of his innings. Assistant Manager Gifford was not too worried by his failure, certain that it was only a matter of time before his considerable appetite for runs curbed his early impetuosity.

The captain's batting problems are more serious at the moment. David has always been a poor net player but in Bombay, he looked completely at odds with himself in the middle. Usually when he fails, he still manages to look composed and his dismissal surprises us, yet here we expected him to get out at any time: even he seemed resigned to imminent failure: the prospect and the process of batting no longer seemed to excite him. The pundits may soon begin to point to the captaincy for his recent decline just as they did with Ian Botham four years ago: it is however worth recalling that he scored two 170's in Pakistan ten months ago when the captaincy was suddenly thrust upon him because of Bob Willis's illness. Nonetheless, the role of a tour captain is extraordinarily demanding, particularly in India.

The captain is the constant figurehead on tour and it is difficult for him to relax completely even in unguarded moments away from the cricket field. He has the ultimate responsibility for all cricketing decisions with the manager, assistant manager and vice-captain acting as his props. Moreover, in India David, quite properly, has been party to all the discussions about the itinerary – we are now operating on the second revised version. At official functions he must produce, along with the manager, short gracious speeches whilst listening attentively to much longer ones. He is continuously hounded by the press for information, comment and quotes and wherever we appear in public, it is Gower who is first to be submerged by the throng of admirers, autograph hunters and gawkers that appear in hotel lobbies and cricket pavilions. He is also expected to score a few runs.

David does not enjoy all the peripheral duties of the tour captain. He likes to switch off for a while in the company of a few close friends and a carefully selected bottle of claret. He recognises that there is life away from the cricket field; winning Test matches is obviously important but not to the exclusion of everything else, which strikes me as a fairly mature philosophy. In Bombay all the burdens of captaincy appeared to weigh heavily upon his shoulders. However, our performance in the field must have cheered him: for the first time since leaving England, we bowled a side out for 180 – thanks to excellent swing bowling from Richard Ellison, quickly rebounding from a disappointing first Test, and the contrasting wiles of Edmonds and Pocock.

Thirty-eight days after leaving England, Martyn Moxon made his debut in an England sweater: he had to wait until the 39th before his first innings. With one over left on the first day, the gallant Pat

Pocock was elevated to open the batting for England (not for the first time) and he survived. The following morning he dutifully sacrificed himself (so he said) to allow Martyn to resume his rightful role at the head of the batting order. Martyn clipped his first ball to the square leg boundary and for the rest of the morning session batted with the aplomb we expect of Yorkshire opening batsmen. Everyone was delighted, especially in view of his ill-starred beginning to the tour.

In Delhi he endured with the rest of us the uncertainties about the future of the tour with the added knowledge that after his first Test selection to face the West Indies at Lord's in 1984, he was forced to withdraw because of a rib injury. In Colombo he acquired a 'Delhi belly' and was confined to his bed whilst we played four days cricket and then came the tragic news of his father's death. Throughout all the disappointments and grief, he remained remarkably calm and phlegmatic though he did confide to the vice-captain that after hearing of his father's death, 'It just doesn't seem as if I'm destined to play'. Martyn knew of his father's illness before leaving England but even though his death was half-expected, 'it was still a shock'.

Back in Barnsley, his family and friends were extremely supportive, urging him to return to India as soon as possible – 'My mum wanted me to come back and I know my dad would have done', and despite all the upsets Martyn himself was eager to return. After such a disastrous start who could have blamed him if he didn't? However, he was inevitably confined to the nets for a fortnight as the First Test was imminent and there was little chance of him being selected since his last innings was at the beginning of September. When Pocock was promoted at Bombay he felt a twinge of disappointment; like a true Yorkshireman, his heart was set upon opening for England, a distinction which he was deprived of for two weeks. In retrospect, he agreed that this decision averted a possible disaster which the pressmen would have seized upon. Of course he was nervous before his first innings yet outwardly he remained composed. 'It was on a par with my debut for Yorkshire. I was apprehensive. I wanted to do well not least for everybody back home.'

Every new tourist is apprehensive prior to departure. Before my first tour (to Australia in 1982/3), I imagined that the rest of the party were stunned by my selection – I was pretty surprised – and I believed that they must be whispering to one another 'whatever is HE doing here?' My confidence and subsequent performances suffered as a result. In fact I am now convinced that tourists do not question the cricketing merit of their colleagues after departure.

They may raise an eyelid in September immediately after the announcement of the party but when we reach Heathrow the topic is irrelevant. Several of our newcomers have admitted to this feeling of insecurity at the outset.

Another major concern is whether you will fit in with your new colleagues and who your friends will be. Martyn is a typical example: 'I knew most people to say "hello" to, but I wasn't very good friends with one particular person.' Happily by Bombay any of his fears were alleviated. Richard Ellison was in a similar situation; apart from Chris Cowdrey and Paul Downton, colleagues at Tonbridge and Exeter University respectively, he knew the others by name alone. 'With the rest for the first couple of weeks, I tended to sit back, stay quiet and let the likes of Allan Lamb do the talking, to try to muck in slowly. Not knowing the individuals you can't tell how they'll react to your jibes. With the management I would speak only when spoken to.' Richard's first impressions of Norman Gifford were similar to those of Tim Robinson, one of extreme wariness, and yet by Bombay Richard was sufficiently confident to reveal to us all his singing talents, even if the lyrics far outweighed the melody in entertainment value.

A perennial problem that haunts the likes of Martyn Moxon, Bruce French, Neil Foster and myself is not being in the Test side. This results in endless net sessions with the admirable Gifford and very few opportunities in the middle. Last winter Chris Tavare had one innings in a one-day international in six and a half weeks: so far here Martyn Moxon has had three days cricket and Bruce French six. It is obviously frustrating being a permanent spectator and it poses new problems for a professional cricketer. Fortunately Martyn Moxon is an excellent net player, but not everyone is. 'You have to play properly if you're ever going to succeed in the middle: for a quarter of an hour you have to really apply your mind.' When a game finally arrives, there is additional pressure to perform well; it may provide your only chance for three weeks. Moreover, the zonal games are usually poorly attended so whilst the 'Test' players relax a little after the rigours of international cricket, five players are desperately trying to prove themselves and stake a claim for future selection. To maintain sanity throughout these long periods of inactivity requires tolerance, patience and a sense of humour.

However, all these irritants become totally insignificant as we read our morning newspapers. At Bhopal 500 miles from Bombay almost 3000 people have died as a result of a leakage of poisonous gas (methyl isocyanate) from a multinational pesticide manufacturing plant. Thousands more are threatened with the possibility of blindness for life – all this despite the claim of the factory chief, 'our safety measures are the best in the country'. 'The Daily', an English tabloid printed in Bombay, didn't mince its words, 'The multi-national bastards of Union Carbide had transformed the entire city into a Nazi concentration camp'. The old city of Bhopal has now become a ghost town as thousands evacuate initially through fear and then by compulsion as attempts are made to burn off the remainder of the poisonous gas.

A United Nations environment department has estimated that about 22,000 people die every year in the developing countries from the use of pesticides no longer manufactured in the West. Large multinationals, operating in the Third World, use different standards to those used in America (for instance) as developing countries, in order to encourage industrialisation and the creation of more jobs, are all too willing to relax rules for these companies. An organic farmer friend of mine, a founder member of the newly formed charity 'Land Heritage', will have been horrified by the pictures and the details of this tragedy, taking solace only from the fact that people will surely become more aware of the dangers of widespread use of pesticides, both to the soil and to human beings.

It is remarkable that almost 10,000 inhabitants have died from unnatural causes since our arrival and yet life seems to continue as normal. Maybe this could only happen in India.

INDIA v ENGLAND (FIRST ONE-DAY INTERNATIONAL)

Played at Nehru Stadium, Poona. December 5
Toss ENGLAND ENGLAND won by 4 wickets

INDIA

K. Srikkanth	b Edmonds	50
*S. M. Gavaskar	b Foster	0
D. B. Vengsarkar	b Ellison	105
S. M. Patil	run out	2
Yashpal Sharma	c Ellison b Foster	37
R. J. Shastri	c Ellison b Foster	11
R. M. H. Binny	not out	0
†K. S. More		
M. Prabhakar	did not bat	
C. Sharma		
R. S. Ghai		
Extras	(LB2 W7)	9
Total	(6 wkts 45 Overs)	214

Fall of Wickets: 1–1, 2–119, 3–126, 4–189, 5–212, 6–214.
Bowling: Cowans 8–0–32–0; Foster 10–0–44–3; Ellison 7–0–45–1; Marks 10–0–48–0; Edmonds 10–0–43–1.

ENGLAND

G. Fowler	c Yashpal b C. Sharma	5
R. T. Robinson	lbw b Ghai	15
M. W. Gatting	not out	115
A. J. Lamb	c and b Prabhakar	3
V. J. Marks	run out	31
*D. I. Gower	c Shastri b Binny	3
R. M. Ellison	run out	4
†P. R. Downton	not out	27
P. H. Edmonds		
N. A. Foster	did not bat	
N. G. Cowans		
Extras	(LB8 NB4)	12
Total	(6 wkts 43.2 Overs)	215

Fall of Wickets: 1–14, 2–43, 3–47, 4–114, 5–117, 6–129.
Bowling: C. Sharma 8.2–0–50–1; Prabhakar 10–1–27–1; Ghai 9–0–38–1; Shastri 8–0–49–0; Binny 8–0–43–1.
Umpires: S. Banerjee and Mohammed Ghouse.

Indira Gandhi lying in state

The Funeral Pyre

A mourner at the funeral

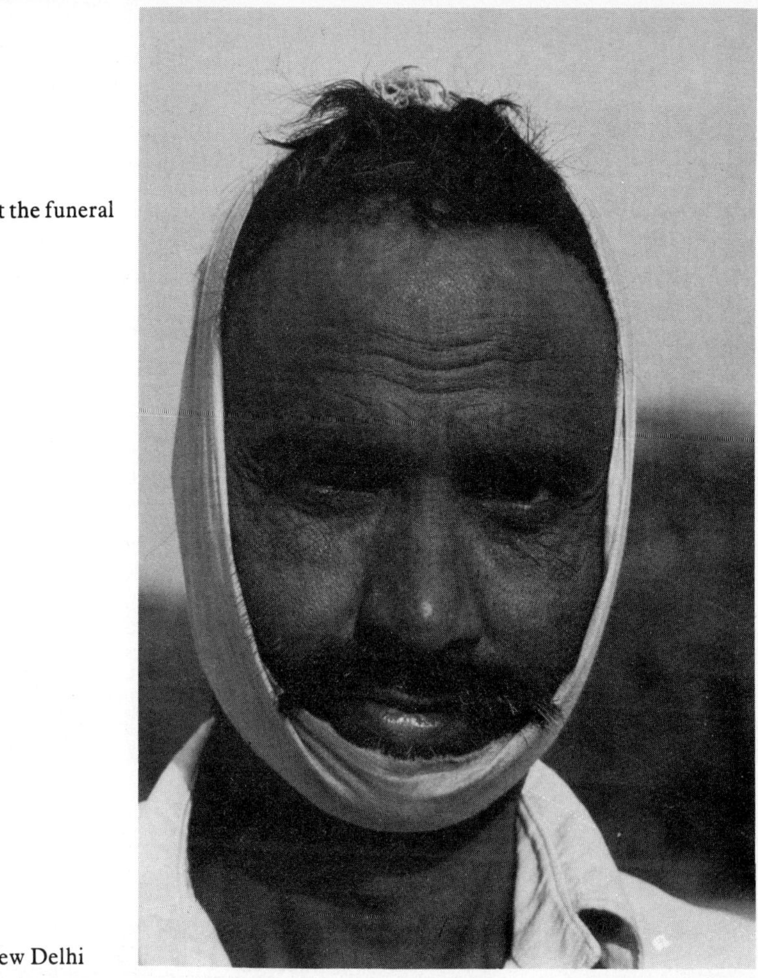

Sikhs in New Delhi

The aftermath, two burnt-out coaches

B. Ganguli and Swarup Kishan pose just before the start of the First Test at the Wankede Stadium in Bombay; December 1984.

Stretching in the hotel grounds

Wherever England travelled in India crowds assembled, especially at the One-Day Internationals. Bangalore, India v. England; January 1985.

Net practice in Delhi before the Second Test, December 1984

Most Test series witness the debut of promising newcomers – none more so than L. Sivaramakrishnan, the 18-year-old leg spinner. He took 12–108, six in each innings, in the First Test.

Mohammed Azharuddin was the other promising debutant. He scored three successive centuries in his first three Tests.

Dilip Vengsarkar on his way to a century in the Fifth Test at Kanpur

The One-Day International at Poona. November 1984

Kapil Dev, the deposed Indian captain, gives David Gower cause for concern during the Second Test.

Sunil Gavaskar, wearing an England cap, looks, understandably, dejected at the end of the Fifth Test at Kanpur. The draw gave England a 2–1 win in the series.

L. Sivaramakrishnan

Richard Ellison

Norman Cowans

Neil Foster

NORTH ZONE v ENGLAND XI

Played at Wankhede Stadium, Bombay. December 7, 8, 9

Toss: ENGLAND XI Match Drawn

NORTH ZONE

C. P. S. Chalihan	lbw b Ellison	24	c French b Foster	8
†S. C. Khanna	c and b Foster	12		
N. S. Sidhu	c French b Foster	0		
A. Malhotra	run out	47	not out	50
Yashpal Sharma	c French b Pocock	22	not out	26
Kirti Azad	c Moxon b Pocock	0		
Gursharan Singh	c and b Edmonds	0	(3) lbw b Marks	53
*S. Madan Lal	run out	42		
M. Prabhakar	c Lamb b Ellison	30	(2) b Foster	31
R. S. Ghai	lbw b Ellison	0		
Maninder Singh	not out	4		
Extras	(B2 LB3)	5	(B1 LB6 W1)	8
Total		186	(3 wkts)	176

Fall of Wickets:
1st Innings: 1–15, 2–15, 3–51, 4–99, 5–99, 6–106, 7–107, 8–175, 9–175, 10–186.
2nd Innings: 1–40, 2–51, 3–118.

Bowling:
1st Innings: Foster 22–4–58–2; Ellison 19.1–9–29–3; Cowdrey 9–3–24–0; Edmonds 14–4–36–1; Pocock 14–4–34–2.
2nd Innings: Foster 8–0–50–2; Ellison 8–3–19–0; Cowdrey 7–0–19–0; Marks 10–3–14–1; Edmonds 13–2–37–0; Pocock 9–3–30–0; Lamb 1–1–0–0.

ENGLAND XI

P. I. Pocock	c Sidhu b Ghai	2
R. T. Robinson	c Malhotra b Maninder	138
M. D. Moxon	lbw b Ghai	42
*D. I. Gower	lbw b Ghai	7
A. J. Lamb	c Prabhakar b Maninder	20
C. S. Cowdrey	lbw b Prabhakar	70
V. J. Marks	c Madan Lal b Ghai	19
R. M. Ellison	b Ghai	10
P. H. Edmonds	b Ghai	15
†B. N. French	lbw b Ghai	19
N. A. Foster	not out	22
Extras	(B3 LB6 NB4)	13
Total		377

Fall of Wickets: 1–3, 2–104, 3–123, 4–158, 5–282, 6–292, 7–305, 8–331, 9–342, 10–377.
Bowling: Prabhakar 17–5–49–1; Ghai 27–4–110–7; Madan Lal 11–1–30–0; Maninder 31–4–107–2; Kirti Azad 14–1–48–0; Chalihan 2–0–24–0.
Umpires: R. Mehra and V. Raju.

7
Delhi

'Dull, dreary, drowsy and spineless' was the Indian TV commentator's description of the first day's play in the Second Test match at Delhi. Come back Jim Laker, all is forgiven. For me the first four days were always absorbing whilst the last one was utterly riveting, especially since I'm English.

When we arrived at the Kotla ground for net practice on the eve of the match, everyone wandered out to the square to go through the normal routine of poking, prodding and passing judgement on the wicket. We were amazed by what we saw. The playing surface was entirely devoid of grass, which was no surprise, but there was also a mosaic of cracks and around them the soil was definitely loose. Despite losing the First Test, we appeared to have a result wicket on our hands, which must surely assist the spinners. Nonetheless, we were pleased by our observations. At least we had an unexpected chance to level the series or go 2–0 down. John Thicknesse, the newshound of the *London Evening Standard*, sought Sunil Gavaskar's opinion.

'Have you seen the Taj Mahal?' asked Sunil mysteriously.

'Yes,' replied Thicknesse.

'Well, if you want to make a return visit, book up on the fourth or fifth day of the Test match.'

The selectors chose the eleven who played at Bombay plus myself, giving themselves the option of playing three spinners. Obviously the final choice was between Chris Cowdrey and myself: we were rooming together in Delhi and we both agreed not to sabotage the other's fitness by rearranging the furniture and turning off the lights.

We discussed the possibilities of the morrow but there was no friction between us and indeed there seldom is in such situations. Any anger or venom at omission is usually reserved for the captain and his selectors, which is a far more logical reaction.

We travelled to the ground by different routes every day – I presume the assassination of Percy Norris had shaken any complacency from our security officers and this scheme was an additional precaution. I arrived not necessarily expecting to play, but having tried hard to convince myself that I would – just in case. We always travel to and from the ground in cricket kit so within minutes we are gathered in a circle doing our stretching exercises with Bernard. Whilst the captain, vice-captain and Giff stare at the wicket again and deliberate amongst themselves, I keep watching them out of the corner of my eye. Surely they've made up their minds by now – the wicket hasn't changed since yesterday. Eventually, the captain moves towards us as we are completing our final exercise. Is he heading for Cowdrey or me? He knows we are both glancing at him, anxious to learn of our destiny over the next six days. Yet he doesn't seem to be walking towards either of us. He goes over to Richard Ellison five yards to my right. Surely they can't be thinking of going into a Test match with one front line seamer? My right eardrum strains hard.

'Elly, is your back all right?' Richard mumbles that it is and the captain moves to his left towards me.

'Sorry you won't be playing.'

'O.K.'

The trepidation at the prospect of playing in a Test match suddenly vanishes to be replaced by a few moments of utter deflation, then resignation at the thought of five days spectating, carrying drinks and bowling at Martyn Moxon. I suppose not playing is an easy option; there will be none of the highs and lows that drain the mind and body during a Test match, just safe mundanity. The decision is announced and a few players quietly express their sympathy and surprise. However, I remain stoic, attempt to catch some of Giff's skiers and being the good tourist, wander over to the nets to bowl at our early order batsmen. Spectating is frustrating. Each day I pack a book, some letter writing material and a note book for this diary yet everything remains in my bag all day. The first Test of a series, no matter how dull the cricket, always commands attention. Thereafter it depends upon the game and at Delhi the feeling that there was always going to be a result made it a compelling Test match to watch. The non-players strenuously avoid passing judgement on their colleagues, certainly not in public; we all know how easy the game is from the stands. Yet when Pat Pocock comes on to bowl I watch more intently, transporting myself into his situation; I examine the field placings minutely and speculate whether I could match his performance.

The Kotla ground is less claustrophobic than the Wankhede Stadium in Bombay: the more expensive stands climb gently into the distance with the result that the atmosphere was more relaxed than what we expected of an Indian Test match especially since there were no more than 7000 spectators present. Tony Lewis, England's captain in 1972/3, recalled the Test grounds being packed and feeling like a cooped chicken as he strode out to bat down the wired tunnel that leads to the arena in Delhi. On 12 December, only the cheapest terracing was filled. Several reasons were offered for this apparent decline in interest – the forthcoming elections, the absence of Botham, the advent of one-day cricket in India and the introduction of televised cricket coverage. We were assured that if they don't come to Calcutta after Christmas, they won't come anywhere.

Gavaskar won the toss and unsurprisingly chose to bat. This time five minutes before the start, Norman Cowans was ushered out of the dressing room with Bruce French to bowl on the outfield. This exercise proved worthwhile as Norman's first spell was straight and hostile yet it was Richard Ellison who made an early breakthrough with a perfect outswinger which Sunil edged to Paul Downton, Gavaskar's fourth consecutive failure against the tourists.

Cowans quickly hit Vengsarkar on the helmet and gained several moral victories without managing to dismiss him. Vengsarkar's approach to batting against Cowans is similar to that of Greg Chappell in Australia in 1982/3; he simply attempts to hit him out of the attack and there is a surprising hint of desperation in his approach for such an experienced and accomplished Test batsman. Edmonds bowling into the sun in a baseball type hat (suitably adorned with England's touring motif) and Pocock were soon introduced and they extracted considerable turn, which increased our doubts about the wicket. In quick succession, Vengsarkar was stumped off Edmonds aiming to hit him through the on side and Gaekwad was bowled by Pocock driving loosely.

After lunch, the spinners continued and the low bounce and slow turn coupled with the accuracy of an elder statesman ensured that India's progress was restrained. There were few of the flamboyant shots of the Bombay Test and even Sandip Patil was subdued and circumspect. Finally Patil's patience snapped and he skied a catch to mid wicket off the persevering Edmonds and with Pocock dismissing Shastri and Amarnath, England found themselves in command at tea-time with the score at 140–6, a position beyond our pre-match expectations. However, after tea, Kapil Dev counterattacked a la Botham with some shots searing to the boundary, others just eluding the fielders' outstretched arms and with Kirmani, who for all his apparent frailties is proving a considerable nuisance in this series, took India to 208 for 6 at the close. The Englishmen felt reasonably satisfied with their day's work though Kent's new captain, who knows when to double at backgammon, reckoned that we would happily swap positions with the Indians, such was our concern about the wicket.

However, for the next three days we waited for the pitch to deteriorate but it steadfastly refused to do so. Each day developed a pattern. In the morning the ball would swing and seam a little despite no obvious signs of moisture but in the final session (3.00–4.30) no wickets fell on the first four days. The bounce was certainly uneven but if anything the ball turned less as the match progressed and those ominous cracks grew no larger. The pitch had deceived all the Indian sages – Pataudi, Gavaskar as well as our coach driver.

On the second morning Richard Ellison removed Kapil and Kirmani within half an hour but we encountered problems with Prabhakar, a swing bowler who had replaced Chetan Sharma, Yadav and Siva. They took the Indian total to 307. Siva at number eleven walks to the crease better than Kevin Jarvis and twiddles his bat better than Kevin Jarvis and he is certainly a better player than Kevin Jarvis as one first class century testifies. If Siva's bowling can guarantee a place in the Indian side, I suspect that he will be batting at 6 or 7 within four years. In fact every player in the Indian side at Delhi looked a capable batsman. Initially our spinners grew impatient at the tailend resistance, summoning extra close fieldsmen in expectation of finishing off the innings with customary speed. Pat Pocock, however, soon realised that these tailenders were imposters and that they would have to be winkled out as if middle order batsmen so the field went back and the bowlers preyed on the batsmen's patience.

With 40 overs left (sensibly both sides have agreed to playing a minimum of 80 overs per day – a target which has not yet proved too burdensome), England began poorly, losing Fowler to an outswinger from Prabhakar. His dismissal relieved me of one of the more unusual and least onerous duties of the twelfth man. Because the players' viewing balcony is so distant from the playing area at Delhi, the captain requested someone to sit and talk with our number three Mike Gatting at the boundary's edge. I volunteered and I can't remember whether we were talking about Congress Party's chances of re-election or Tottenham's climb up the first division when our conversation was rudely interrupted. Whatever it was, Gatting's mind was swiftly atuned to the art of batting until the last over before tea when he pushed forward to Yadav with exaggerated care: the ball hit the middle of his bat but trickled gently onto his off stump – 60–2. After the break, Allan Lamb joined Tim Robinson and on this occasion decided simply to occupy the crease, mindful of previous failures. He got off the mark with a pulled four against Siva and thereafter scored eight runs in eighty minutes, a most uncharacteristic display but valuable not only for his own confidence but also for the team. By the close, we had progressed to 107–2 and the match was beautifully poised.

With a mixture of pride and shame I inform you that I drank for England on the rest day. In Delhi we were inundated with offers of hospitality, some of which could not be refused, so along with the indefatigable Norman Gifford, I flew the flag at four separate functions – a career best. Obviously the management and the non-players are the first to be volunteered for these duties and when we finally crept to bed, we pondered briefly upon the quality of net practice that we would provide for our batsmen at 8.30 next morning. As we travelled towards our luncheon appointment, we noted the difference between New Delhi and the other centres which we had visited so far – wide tree-lined roads, open parks and the absence of hovels and beggars, India's equivalent to Canberra and Milton Keynes (except that the signposts are more comprehensible). We were told that we were visiting a farm on the outskirts of Delhi but when we arrived we found a mansion, built on a three-acre plot, which nourished three rows of cabbages and potatoes at one corner, thereby ensuring tax relief for its owner.

There we met a film actor of Orson Welles proportions (physically) and we learned that the Indian Film Industry is a prosperous one, only recently threatened by the advent of television and video. A few years ago, a villager might spend a week's wages to travel all day to his nearest major city, see the latest film and arrive home to be feted by his fellows as a great adventurer. No doubt, the Indian Film Industry will feel the pinch that afflicted British Film makers in the

60's and 70's but the widespread ownership of TV's and videos will take some more time yet and our 'Orson' was not too perturbed about his future.

Later on our travels, which encompassed Fosters at the Australian High Commission and Steak and Kidney pie at the British High Commission, I was delighted to meet Abbas Ali Baig. Abbas played for India, but, even better, for Oxford and Somerset. He was amazed to hear that Bill Alley had stopped playing, let alone umpiring and that Ken Palmer's son now played in the county side. Abbas, who was providing expert comments for Peter Baxter's Test Match Special team, predicted that the Delhi Test would be drawn; his charming wife however, uncluttered by too much technical knowledge, assured me categorically that there would be a result.

One journalist was tempted to begin his report on Saturday's play 'England batted all day at Delhi without losing a wicket, yet ended the day at 337–5.' More umpiring problems, I'm afraid.

Let me concentrate first on the three batsmen dismissed. Allan Lamb, whilst guarding against fatal overambition, played with greater fluency and assurance than on Thursday evening. After ninety minutes he had reached his first fifty of the series when he pushed forward defensively to an offspinner from Yadav, the ball ricocheted into the hands of Vengsarkar at silly point, who appealed vigorously and successfully. It had been propelled there from the middle of Allan's front pad. Enter Gower under pressure, weighed down by previous failures. Before play began he had looked back to his best in the nets for the first time on tour, not just because Gifford and I may have been slightly under par. All the bowlers had nodded to one another that this was the true David Gower; even his defensive shots were skimming back past the bowler. In the last over before lunch, Siva around the wicket bowled him a shortish leg break which was kept low. David tried to turn it to square leg, missed it and was adjudged lbw. Watching the TV replay, I studied the position of Kirmani behind the stumps and noticed him moving way down the leg side. This was David's second dubious decision in three Test innings and his third of the tour. It is difficult to regain your touch in such circumstances.

After lunch, Chris Cowdrey batted for an hour and produced a gem of an innings, notable for its lack of inhibition. After an uncertain start he played as if he was wearing a Kent sweater: he advanced down the wicket to pull drive Yadav for six and then hoisted Siva over the long-on boundary. The Indian spinners were clearly rattled by such treatment; Siva lost the bounce in his approach to the wicket and Gavaskar quickly removed two of his close catchers whilst the more experienced Yadav immediately flattened his trajectory. Suddenly they appeared vulnerable. Cowdrey had taken the bold option by his determination to play his own way, risking looking a complete imbecile if he miscued a big drive straight up into the air. This is one of the qualities that has made Ian Botham the cricketer that he is – the refusal to settle for safe mediocrity. Cowdrey is no Botham, of course, but his approach on this occasion was equally positive. However, on 38 he was caught at slip off his boot from the bowling of Siva; again the second dubious decision in three Test innings.

Despite these three setbacks we managed to end the day in a commanding position thanks to Tim Robinson aided in the final 2½ hours by the adhesive Paul Downton. Tim's innings left everyone searching for superlatives.

I've already compared him to a passive Gooch, now in terms of application and patience add Boycott – not a bad combination. He displayed so many virtues; he was utterly unflappable either by occasional false strokes or the decisions of the umpires, which he later declared strengthened his resolve to keep going. His batting bears the hallmark of a qualified accountant; it is highly organized, efficient with no unnecessary frills and on this occasion produced the right figures. Like most top batsmen he plays to a definite pattern and it becomes simple to predict his favourite range of scoring shots. He relishes seamers bowling at his leg stump as he times the ball superbly through square leg whilst spinners, if short, will be clipped square on the off side with surprising power. His demeanour at the wicket is passive, almost ponderous for such a fleet-footed man and increasingly it suggests an air of permanence. Already he has proved to be an inspired selection. When he returned to the dressing room there were no dramatic leaps of delight (I suppose he had been batting for six hours) just a quiet smile and a clear resolution to get some more runs. As Bruce French observed, 'He's ideally suited to Test Match cricket because he just loves batting.'

Indeed it required an unplayable lifter from Kapil Dev on the fourth morning to dismiss him and thereafter the English innings lost its momentum. For the third successive time, Siva took six wickets in an innings but he had not been the same destructive force of Bombay. Here he polished off the tail as England acquired a lead of 111 – Nelson, maybe a good omen – thanks to Paul Downton. Paul's innings are rarely memorable; he nudges, pushes and sweeps Knott style and just occasionally unleashes a rasping cover drive but they have been of immense value on this tour. He is a model professional, conscientious about his own fitness and performance and despite being a shy retiring character a great encourager of bowlers and fielders from behind the stumps.

Cowans, having recovered from a stomach upset, again launched a fierce assault upon India's openers and Prabhakar, who was promoted because Gaekwad was ill, was dismissed by a classic piece of modern fast bowling. He just managed to avoid two vicious short balls but was obviously unsettled: the third ball was of fuller length wide of the off stump and Prabhakar drove at it, firm-footed, and nicked it to the wicketkeeper. Again Vengsarkar was ill at ease against Cowans, which was surprising considering his excellent record against the West Indies, and soon in a belated attempt to remove his bat from the line of the ball, he played on. Norman continued to pummel Gavaskar with short deliveries and the Indian captain looked distinctly uncomfortable: instead of swaying or ducking, an art which he has mastered over the years, he allowed the ball to hit his body.

However, Amarnath was utterly untroubled. He hooked Cowans for six to get off the mark and then cover drove him for four persuading Gower to remove Cowans from the attack. Thereafter, Gavaskar also looked more relaxed. Chris Cowdrey, who was fielding at forward short leg, observed that the more he talked to Sunil, the better he played. As the sun dropped, the batsmen protested that the shadows of the close fieldsmen were affecting their concentration. The debate between Gower, the umpires and the batsmen continued for several minutes: no doubt the shadows were a slight inconvenience, but the situation also presented the Indians with a golden opportunity to waste time. Finally this protracted discussion ended with all parties satisfied whereupon Gavaskar inquired of Cowdrey, 'Sorry is my shadow disturbing you also?' I suspect that the mischievous streak in Sunil's character is coming more to the fore in the twilight of his career. Indeed during the penultimate over of the day, he launched a sudden assault upon Pat Pocock. Having proceeded with all the restraint that India's plight demanded, he suddenly leapt down the wicket to pull drive Pocock for 6 and 4; this was followed by an imperious square cut: it was as if he was officially announcing that the drought was ended and that he was back in form.

However, on the fifth morning, after Amarnath had been bowled in Edmonds' first over, Gavaskar's concentration wavered and he fell to Pocock attempting to cut a straight ball. England's spinners now applied extreme pressure on the new batsmen presenting few scoring opportunities, Pocock varying his flight cleverly whilst Edmonds' trajectory was flatter and unrelenting. Yet Patil and Shastri survived until lunch – Patil lofting the last ball into the stands at long on taking the score to 204–5, a lead of 95.

Our chances of victory appeared to be fading and this was reflected in the mood of the players in the dressing room; it was one of anger rather than optimism. A convincing bat/pad appeal against Patil had just been rejected and even the philosophical Pocock was enraged. The two spinners had deserved greater rewards after their morning's toil. The new ball was due and there was a discussion as to whether it was worthwhile for Norman Cowans to share it with Phil Edmonds. Perhaps the harder ball would bounce more for the spinners, who represented our only realistic chance of winning the match. Eventually it was decided to persevere with the old ball for twenty minutes; if nothing happened Norman would be summoned for one last effort.

Immediately after lunch, Bruce French, Norman Gifford and myself went to the nets, which gave us no view of the cricket, although we could see one of the scoreboards. After twenty minutes we had abandoned our practice and were scurrying back to the pavilion as four wickets had fallen and the game was alight. I apologise, dear reader, for having missed the most crucial phase of the Test and perhaps the tour, but when Gifford calls we must respond. Clearly I am not suited to cricket journalism – a true reporter would never have admitted his absence. However, an animated Tony Brown provided us with the details.

Sandip Patil fell in identical fashion to the first innings attempting to hit Edmonds to mid wicket but only striking the ball to Allan Lamb. Kapil Dev struts to the wicket. He played loosely at his first ball, flicking it straight to square cover; his second was defended and the third was whipped off the stumps to square leg – one run and the end of the over. Now Kapil galloped down the wicket to Pocock's first ball and clubbed it into the stands at long on; the next was flighted and a little wider, again Kapil advanced down the wicket intent on repeating the shot, he miscued into the safe hands of Allan Lamb – the end of an innings of startling irresponsibility. Englishmen looking on mumbled that 'not even Botham on a bad day would have . . .'

Now the Indians were under severe pressure. In quick succession

Gaekwad snicked Edmonds to the wicketkeeper and Kirmani played back to a good length offspinner and was bowled. Crowds began to filter into the stadium from the streets of Delhi sensing a dramatic finish from their transistor radios. Shastri remained resolute but was unable to puncture the deep set field whilst Yadav blocked, the dismissals of Patil and Kapil Dev rendering any bold counterattack unthinkable. Half an hour of tense cricket ensued as the English spinners offered no respite to the batsmen: numerous appeals were rejected; the fielders couldn't hide their frustration but Edmonds and Pocock remained patient and controlled. Eventually Yadav was brilliantly caught in the gully by Lamb off Edmonds and the Indians again looked to Siva to turn the course of this match – as a batsman. He dawdled to the wicket and slowly surveyed the field and for a while kicked Pocock away. Pocock tempted him with several slower flighted deliveries until his aggressive instincts could resist no longer and his attempted straight drive was safely caught by the English off-spinner. England needed 125 to win in just under two hours – an estimated 32 overs.

It cost Graeme Fowler 22 rupees to open the batting for England – the price of a taxi from the Taj Palace Hotel to the Kotla ground. Graeme had spent two days in bed with a mysterious stomach complaint. As wickets tumbled Tony Brown had rung him up to suggest that he should make his way to the ground immediately. There was a swift discussion as to whether he should open: Gower, despite his recent failures, was prepared to do it but Foxy was willing and it was decided to keep the established batting order. Up in the players' viewing box, Gifford fixed himself a large pipe of tobacco and sat down, helpless, to await the outcome. Being an eternal pessimist I suggested that all three results were still possible: of course if this were a John Player League match I would have been supremely confident, but it was a Test match and it's a rare occurrence for Tests to end in a run chase. However, once Fowler and Robinson had survived the first five overs snatching singles at every opportunity, the Indians quickly became demoralised, still stunned by their earlier batting collapse. Even their efforts to waste time were half-hearted. Siva was soon introduced but couldn't produce any miracles this time. The loss of Robinson and Fowler failed to halt England's momentum as Lamb and Gatting batted with massive authority against the spinners, like boxers waiting to deliver the knock out punch. As an English victory became inevitable, the Indian outcricket grew increasingly ragged; Siva bowled two no balls and two high full tosses in one over and even Shastri's clockwork precision went awry. With ten overs remaining, Gavaskar formally conceded defeat by electing to bowl himself and Lamb smote him over mid-on to win the match.

I watched the closing overs from the BBC commentary box. Mike Selvey, who had been fulfilling the Trevor Bailey role in Bombay and Delhi, had been laid low by stomach cramps and a breathless Peter Baxter, the producer, therefore summoned any stray Englishman to replace him. He may have been a trifle disappointed to fall upon me as I had managed to interrupt the 9 o'clock news on my previous excursion into the box.

As victory became more certain, it was heartwarming to witness the excitement of Tony Lewis, the winning captain here in 1972, and such experienced campaigners as Baxter and Michael Carey of the *Daily Telegraph*. I don't suppose either of them have reported many English Test victories overseas.

Everyone was anxious to return to the hotel quickly to relax and mull over our victory, however the bus was delayed by Geoffrey Sanlez, our standard bearer, who was searching for the English flag, and also by David Gower, who was giving the most pleasurable press conference of his career, any personal disappointment about his own form being swept away by the euphoria of victory. Back at the hotel we gathered in the team room where some disgusting Indian champagne arrived, yet it tasted fine: soon BBC TV cameramen urged us to celebrate wildly for the benefit of viewers of the 9 o'clock news and Fowler and Lamb obliged. Yet our real celebrations never bordered on the excessive: we went to the British High Commission's bar, ate English sausages, egg and chips, drank some cans of John Smith's bitter and monopolised the darts board and snooker table. There was a little self-congratulation – quite justified – and so much to be proud of, the marathon innings of Tim Robinson, the big-hearted swing bowling of Richard Ellison in the first innings, the refusal to be daunted by several dubious umpiring decisions, excellent outcricket and the superb pressure bowling of Edmonds and Pocock on the fifth day.

Gradually the significance of our win began to sink in as the ghost of Fletcher's form was exorcised. England had now gained a definite psychological ascendancy in the Test series which was reflected in the aftermath of the match. Gower and Robinson were going tiger hunting for a week in Rajasthan whilst in the Indian camp there were rumours of a dressing room altercation between Gavaskar and Kapil

Dev after Kapil's dismissal. Apparently Kapil and Sandip Patil had been dropped for the one-day international at Cuttack and the Third Test at Calcutta. At first we were suspicious of this news for dropping Kapil is the equivalent of England omitting Botham, something which the selectors may have contemplated over the years, but which they have never dared to do if only because of the psychological boost this action would give the opposition.

The Indians, triumphant and garlanded in Bombay, were suddenly self-destructing and in disarray, whilst the Englishmen's morale had soared to such heights that even the prospect of a 7 o'clock flight next morning was perfectly acceptable.

INDIA v ENGLAND (SECOND TEST MATCH)

Played at Ferozeshah Kotla, New Delhi

December 12, 13, 15, 16, 17

Toss: INDIA   ENGLAND won by 8 wickets

INDIA

*S. M. Gavaskar	c Downton b Ellison	1	b Pocock	65
A. D. Gaekwad	b Pocock	28	(8) c Downton b Edmonds	0
D. B. Vengsarkar	st Downton b Edmonds	24	b Cowans	1
M. Amarnath	c Gower b Pocock	42	b Edmonds	64
S. M. Patil	c Pocock b Edmonds	30	c Lamb b Edmonds	41
R. J. Shastri	c Fowler b Pocock	2	not out	25
Kapil Dev	c Downton b Ellison	60	c Lamb b Pocock	7
†S. M. H. Kirmani	c Gatting b Ellison	27	(9) b Pocock	6
M. Prabhakar	c Downton b Ellison	25	(2) c Downton b Cowans	5
N. S. Yadav	not out	28	c Lamb b Edmonds	1
L. Sivaramakrishnan	run out	25	c and b Pocock	0
Extras	(B1 LB12 NB2)	15	(B6 LB10 W1 NB3)	20
Total		307		235

Fall of Wickets:

1st Innings: 1–3, 2–56, 3–68, 4–129, 5–131, 6–140, 7–208, 8–235, 9–258, 10–307.

2nd Innings: 1–12, 2–15, 3–136, 4–172, 5–207, 6–214, 7–216, 8–225, 9–234, 10–235.

Bowling:

1st Innings: Cowans 20–5–70–0; Ellison 26–6–66–4; Edmonds 44.2–16–83–2; Pocock 33–8–70–3; Gatting 2–0–5–0.

2nd Innings: Cowans 13–2–43–2; Ellison 7–1–20–0; Edmonds 44–24–60–4; Pocock 38.4–9–93–4; Gatting 1–0–3–0.

ENGLAND

G. Fowler	c Gaekwad b Prabhakar	5	c Vengsarkar b Sivaramakrishnan	29
R. T. Robinson	c Gavaskar b Kapil Dev	160	run out	18
M. W. Gatting	b Yadav	26	not out	30
A. J. Lamb	c Vengsarkar b Yadav	52	not out	37
*D. I. Gower	lbw b Sivaramakrishnan	5		
C. S. Cowdrey	c Gavaskar b Sivaramakrishnan	38		
†P. R. Downton	c Kapil Dev b Sivaramakrishnan	74		
P. H. Edmonds	c Shastri b Sivaramakrishnan	26		
R. M. Ellison	b Sivaramakrishnan	10		
P. I. Pocock	b Sivaramakrishnan	0		
N. G. Cowans	not out	0		
Extras	(B6 LB13 NB3)	22	(B4 LB7 NB2)	13
Total		418	(2 wkts)	127

Fall of Wickets:

1st Innings: 1–15, 2–60, 3–170, 4–181, 5–237, 6–343, 7–398, 8–411, 9–415, 10–418.

2nd Innings: 1–41, 2–68.

Bowling:

1st Innings: Kapil Dev 32–5–87–1; Prabhakar 21–3–68–1; Sivaramakrishnan 49.1–17–99–6; Yadav 36–6–95–2; Shastri 29–4–44–0; Amarnath 2–0–6–0.

2nd Innings: Kapil Dev 6–0–20–0; Prabhakar 3–0–18–0; Sivaramakrishnan 8–0–41–1; Yadav 2–0–7–0; Shastri 4–0–20–0; Gavaskar 0.4–0–10–0.

Umpires: D. N. Doti Walla and P. D. Reporter.

8

Gauhati – Christmas – Cuttack

In the cosmopolitan cities of Bombay and Delhi Indian acquaintances kept chuckling when we mentioned that we were going to Gauhati. Our Liaison officers, however, were less amused as they had to scramble around government offices to finalise the special permits, which are requirements for all visitors to Assam and the N.E. of India. We were visiting a sensitive, isolated area for here India meets with Bhutan, China, Burma and Bangladesh and events since 1980 have virtually shut off the region completely. There have been strikes, riots, violence and terrorism as the inhabitants have felt neglected by central government, especially since the north-east provides a large proportion of India's oil without reaping the benefits of this new-found wealth. Even more distressing for the natives of this region has been the massive influx of 'foreigners' from Bangladesh across the lightly guarded borders. In some areas these 'foreigners' actually outnumber the indigenous population and this caused so much unrest in 1983 that there were wholesale massacres in some villages. Since it was deemed impossible for the authorities to establish who was entitled to vote, there were to be no elections in Assam.

Aware of all these problems we had good reason to be a little apprehensive about our trip north and yet trouble never seems to come from the predictable source in India. The atmosphere in Gauhati was less oppressive, less claustrophobic than anywhere we have visited on this tour. The gentle slopes, dotted with palm trees and wooden shacks, were reminiscent of some of the Caribbean islands and so was the tempo of life. Alongside the banks of the broad

Brahmaputra river children flew their kites, played beach cricket and swam whilst their mothers carried out the week's washing. They displayed just a mild detached interest in the curious white visitors armed with instamatics and were a little embarrassed when Foxy removed his lens cap again. Allan Lamb tried to charter a fishing boat but no one could understand him so we settled for a trishaw ride around the town – a rickshaw propelled by a bicycle – an expedition which we would not have contemplated in the congested streets of Bombay.

This decision posed all sorts of moral dilemmas for Paul Downton and myself. We hired three vehicles: Allan and Foxy must have watched Ben Hur on the in-house videos recently since they immediately cajoled their rider to pedal at top speed; they were closely pursued by Marty Moxon and Bruce French. But Paul and myself hired a rider who was either devoid of any competitive instinct or nursing a severe hangover or approaching premature senility. As our companions disappeared into the distance, our man ground to a halt on the slightest of inclines; he dismounted and, crestfallen, started to push the rickshaw along the road. Should we suggest that the superfit Downton pedal and risk denting the poor man's pride? Should we desert him in favour of some up and coming rickshaw operator, thereby depriving him of his evening bowl of rice? Or should we simply get off and walk? Being compassionate, humanitarian types we chose the latter option and when we finally remounted we instructed him to take every available downhill turning until we returned to base. We vied with coaches, cars and lorries for the right of way but at least our safety was never seriously threatened; at that pace a dive to the side of the road would not have proved fatal.

Still, we enjoyed the freedom of being able to discover the city unmolested; there was a notable absence of beggars and when a few of the townsfolk meandered up for autographs they were polite, patient and not the least overbearing – a stark contrast to Poona and Bombay. No one seemed to mind that there would be no elections in Gauhati; just as when the lights went out in our hotel, nobody was in the least bit concerned except Richard Ellison, who was aroused from his early evening nap by candle-lit carol singers in the form of Cowdrey and Marks. To our astonishment – and disgust – no contributions were forthcoming for the Christmas fund from that quarter.

Our party was reduced to twelve players during our stay in

Gauhati. David Gower and Tim Robinson were in Rajasthan looking for tigers. Even before the Delhi Test match it had been mooted that a week's rest would benefit the captain far more than intensive net practice. He desperately needed a break and our victory in Delhi enabled him to have one without any critical comments from the press, 'England in Disarray – Gower on Holiday'. Tim Robinson after his marathon effort at Delhi was rewarded by being asked to accompany him which represented a remarkable elevation in stature within six weeks of being an England player. Paul Allott was now back in Sale supping ale and reintroducing himself to his six-month-old son. For three weeks Paul had been dogged by a mysterious back injury and on the final day of the test it was decided that he should return home for specialist treatment. Amidst the celebrations of our victory Paul could not quite hide his personal disappointment. After a superb summer against the West Indies, he had finally established himself as England's premier seam bowler at the beginning of the tour. Yet now he would have to start that long climb again beginning in February, April, June – who knows? We shall miss his experience of India as well as his sharp, no-nonsense Lancastrian wit. Pat Pocock had been despatched to Calcutta to meet Paul's replacement, Jonathan Agnew, along with his (Pat's) wife and two children. So Richard Ellison, our only twelfth man, who was overdue for a rest, spent his days scurrying hither and thither fetching sweaters, hats and drinks until he declared himself more exhausted at the end of the day than if he'd bowled 25 overs. It's always preferable to be playing on tour.

Let me mention the match briefly, if only because I finally took some wickets. It provided another indication of the growing confidence of this side as we completely outplayed a weak East Zone XI on a poor batting surface. Graeme Fowler provided the backbone of our innings with an excellent century, which proved that his technique against spinners has advanced considerably over the last three years – his nimble footwork is as vital against the spinners as the fast bowlers. In this department alone East Zone provided demanding opposition through left arm spinners Dilip Doshi and Kumar; however, their batting was inept with only Arun Lal, a former tourist to England, offering much resistance in their first innings. The pitch assisted the spin bowlers and initially I became very frustrated by my lack of success. I bowled seven mediocre overs before lunch on the second day, feeling as if I should be taking a wicket every over. This is a familiar trap for a spinner; the wicket is obviously turning and some insensitive idiot in the dressing room blurts out 'you must get six wickets here' and you suddenly find yourself under pressure. After lunch I consciously tried to relax, to concentrate simply upon accuracy and to be patient. Stop the batsmen scoring and wickets are more likely to fall. Lo and behold I took three wickets in nine balls and I suspect my relief was obvious. I finished with a respectable 4–48 from 29 overs. Following on East Zone were bundled out for 52 on the third morning even though we dropped four catches.

This performance earned us an early departure to Calcutta and an extra day to prepare for our Christmas celebrations. No nets would be available there because the authorities were unable to provide any security forces due to the imminent general election. The election also thwarted the Social Committee's plans to buy each member of the touring party a Christmas present as the shops were shut for three days. So Cowdrey and myself laboured into the early hours in order to compensate for this omission by providing additional entertainment for our Christmas party. The Social Committee held several crisis meetings in an effort to ensure that Christmas away from home wasn't utterly depressing for it is then that cricket tourists are most vulnerable to bouts of homesickness. Tony Brown, for instance, was experiencing his first Christmas away from his family and he was not relishing the prospect. Generally everyone musters a grim determination to enjoy themselves.

On Christmas Eve a party of twelve players and journalists attended a midnight communion service at St Paul's Cathedral. It is a salutary thought for those ardent Anglicans at home that there are more practising Christians in India than in the British Isles. Admittedly this represents only 2–3% of the population, yet being a minority religion it suggests a far stronger commitment than in the nominally Christian British Isles. The Church was packed and we were reserved two candlelit pews at the front. The service lasted almost 2 hours; the carol-singing lacked the fervour that most of us yearned for yet the communion itself was similar to our English service and reminded us of the original reason for our celebrations. The sermon was in English but delivered by a Bengali bishop who I could not follow and I soon suffered the indignity of being elbowed in the ribs by the eleven year old Toby Pocock as my eyelids closed.

On Christmas morning Cowdrey and I rushed out to the nearby market to buy a few last minute gifts for our guests at lunch – Stephanie Fowler, Diane Pocock and her daughter Sam, and Toby. We returned in time for our traditional mid-morning drinks party hosted by the press. Chris Lander of the *Daily Mirror* and Graeme Morris, both dressed in Indian waiter's colourful uniform, distributed a hastily concocted punch, whose ingredients remained a guarded secret. The press entertained us with a string of parodies composed by Mike Carey and Peter Baxter such as 'I'm dreaming of Sivaramakrishnan'. Another to be sung to the tune of 'Old Man River' is reproduced here by kind permission of the authors.

GAUHATI/XMAS

Here we all work on the Brahmaputra
Here we will work while the white folk play
Wielding them bats from the dawn till sunset
Getting no rest till the close of play
Don't hook up or put a catch down
Cos that upsets Mr Tony Brown
Play, right forward or get right back
Dat's the only way on this sort of track
Old Man Robbo, that old man Robbo
He must know something, he don't say nothing
He just keeps batting, keeps on batting along
He's not like Gower, he's not like Gatting
For some strange reason he keeps on batting
Dat old man Robbo he just keeps batting along
You and me we sweat and strain
On really good pitches or affected by rain
Defend those stumps and guard that bail
If you get bowled out, you get bollocked by 'The Mail'
We gets weary and sick of tonning
Just like Boycott it's bloody boring
But Old Man Robbo, he just keeps batting along.

We decided that this was probably the best piece that the press had written for a while.

At noon the players left to change into fancy dress and I can report that the British ability to improvise in adversity was soon in evidence. The Social Committee naturally came as the three wise men wearing tablecloths and tea cosies. Several members of the party had endeared themselves to the hotel staff so that Norman Gifford, his normal ruddy complexion disguised by boot polish, arrived as a bearer, Tony Brown as a head waiter, whilst Paul Downton in a security guard's uniform frisked everyone as they entered our dining room. Martyn Moxon was a remarkably convincing Boy George and appropriately Phil Edmonds alighted as an Arab Sheikh with a Barclays Bank cheque book pinned to his chest. However the panel of judges, Mrs Fowler, Mrs Pocock, Sam and Toby, decided upon joint winners. A mud-daubed Allan Lamb looked every inch an Indian beggar apart from a certain lack of servility whilst Neil Foster in a sari raised several eyebrows as he made his way to the gents. Indeed when Father Christmas arrived with presents for the wives and children, we tried to thrust a gift into the arms of Foster, ignoring Diane Pocock who was dressed in full England regalia – white trousers, MCC sweater and cap.

The hotel gallantly tried to provide us with a traditional turkey lunch and their efforts were greatly appreciated. Throughout the meal we dutifully toasted the Queen and absent friends – in particular wives and sweethearts and Paul Allott. Christmas crackers were tugged and a motley selection of wine, carefully reserved for the occasion, was consumed.

Then Chris Cowdrey read out a few Christmas messages for the team that had mysteriously come into his possession. David Gower received a note of congratulations upon winning the Delhi Test from deposed Australian Test Captain Kim Hughes, followed by a plaintive plea for advice. To Pat Pocock – 'hope you are enjoying the tour as much as our first trip together – Percy Fender!' To Martyn Moxon – 'Good luck playing in Calcutta – Watch out for the dogleg Seventeenth – love Boycs'.

After the meal we entertained one another with turns from the new tourists who adapted 'The Twelve Days of Christmas', the captain and vice-captain who conducted an interview on Indian television, and there were two versions of the Selectors meeting in September 1984, one from the Management, one from Cowdrey, Marks and Ellison. I can only recall a few edited highlights of our version. It began with P. B. H. May (Cowdrey) calling the meeting to order, 'Right chaps, we're here to pick a side to tour Pakistan this winter', it continued with Alec Bedser's (Ellison) surprise that Brown (Freddie) had been appointed tour manager and A. C. Smith's (Marks) astonishment at the selection of Fowler (Bill of Derbyshire). Thereafter AC + PBH suggested a whole stream of public schoolboys ranging from Mark Nicholas to Roddy Kinkead Weekes and they were both delighted when Alec suggested Pocock only to be dismayed to learn that he meant Pat of Surrey rather than Nick of Hampshire. (In fact the tour party with the arrival of Agnew contains seven public schoolboys.) The meeting ended in disarray when

Alec stormed out in disgust at the prospect of a Parisian keeping wicket for England, 'As for the wicketkeeper he's French'. Finally PBH rang up Colin Cowdrey to assure him 'I've got the lad in'. In case anyone high and mighty reads this I would like to emphasise that the sketch was intended to be funny rather than to represent the truth and that I'm still available for future selection.

By four o'clock the party had broken up and many of us withdrew to our rooms to attempt, with varying degrees of success, to make telephone calls to loved ones in England. In a sense Christmas on tour resembles an obstacle course, something to survive with the minimum of discomfort. We feel obliged to enjoy ourselves yet we would all prefer to be shivering in our own homes. At least there were no obvious casualties in Calcutta.

On Boxing Day we resumed our lives as cricketers after four days break, practising in the morning before flying to Bhubaneswar for the second one-day international at Cuttack. Already we sensed the heightened enthusiasm for cricket in Bengal. As we boarded the bus outside the Grand Hotel in Calcutta, crowds ten deep stood on tiptoe to catch a glimpse of the tourists and on arrival in Bhubaneswar a strong police cordon was necessary to ensure an easy passage to our hotel. The following day, 27 December, was a long one, beginning with a 7.30 a.m. departure from Bhubaneswar, which was an hour's drive from Cuttack and ending with a 9.30 p.m. flight back to Calcutta. In between there was plenty of drama.

The cricket stadium at Cuttack, in contrast to the town itself, is a magnificent sight with spacious seating for 35,000 spectators, a lush green outfield and an excellent wicket. It might provide an ideal venue for the projected World Cup in 1987 if the nearest respectable hotel was not an hour's drive away. After hastily completing our pre-match preparations, Gower won the toss and took to the field with the same eleven that won at Poona. For two hours our outcricket was below par maybe because of our recent lay off over Christmas, or the morning's rushed coach trip or simply the excellence of the Indian openers, Srikanth and Shastri, who had been promoted instead of Gavaskar. They amassed 186 together in contrasting styles. Srikanth is a spectator's dream, even though he has apparently tempered the carefree aggression, which characterised his innings against Fletcher's tourists. You can tell that he shuns orthodoxy even before he takes strike as he ambles out to the wicket wearing paper-thin tennis shoes and swinging a bat that might easily have been purloined from Ottery St Mary CC's kit bag. At the start of his innings he looks distinctly insecure, slashing wildly outside the off stump, flailing at bouncers, whereupon he may suddenly loft the opening bowler over mid off with the authority of Harold Gimblett. Thereafter he can be a nightmare for fielding captains since it is impossible to predict his next move. At Cuttack I bowled to him with four boundary fielders and he was quite prepared to try to clear them, whether this was a conscious decision or sheer exuberance it is difficult to tell. He hit me for two sixes straight over Graeme Fowler's head at deep mid-wicket forcing Gower to turn to Gatting's medium pace. In limited overs games my boundary fielders are my chief deterrents and when they are disdainfully ignored, it is time for a rest. Afterwards Norman Gifford suggested that I might have introduced more variations of pace and flight to keep him guessing rather than bowl consistently flat so that he could set himself for his favourite thumps in the certain knowledge of where and when the ball would land. It is a strategy that has brought some success against New Zealand's arch slogger, Lance Cairns, but at Cuttack Srikanth's onslaughts were executed so swiftly that I lacked the confidence and the rhythm to strive for much variety so early in my spell.

Meanwhile, Shastri, neat, determined and thoroughly professional, advanced in more conventional style at the other end. However when Srikkanth was adjudged lbw to Gatting on 99 the Indian innings began to lose its momentum. Shastri was keen to notch a century whilst Vengsarkar, Sharma and Binny took precious overs to acclimatise as England's outcricket grew sharper. The problems of India's middle order batsmen reminded me of a remark of Bill Alley, Somerset's trusty all-rounder of the 60's. A colleague was suggesting to Bill that Tom Graveney was the complete batsman, eulogising at length about his graceful style, his powers of concentration and his exquisite timing. Yet despite all this evidence Bill remained unconvinced, finally retorting, 'Ah, but he can't slog'. Well, so far in the one-day internationals the Indians have not been adept at 'slogging' in the last ten overs of their innings. Here they finished with 252 off 49 overs, a stiff target but not an unattainable one.

In reply England stuttered to 140–5, Mike Gatting, brimful of confidence, scoring 58 before being bowled cutting off spinner Ashok Patel whilst David Gower had looked rehabilitated after hitting four crisp boundaries until he smashed a long hop to deep mid wicket. Yet with Downton and Marks fresh at the crease and with 110 required off 18 overs the situation was bordering upon the critical. At least we had both been in similar positions for our respective counties on numerous occasions, which enabled us to realise that the situation was not irretrievable and that it would be counterproductive to cast all caution to the winds against the Indian spinners Ravi Shastri and Patel. Nonetheless, we needed some boundaries, which meant taking a few calculated risks. Once the required run rate exceeds six an over in limited overs games there comes a time when the batsman has to brace himself, depart from his normal method of batting and say to himself, 'Here we go! Hope this works because I'm going to look an imbecile if it doesn't'. This decision was reflected in two shots, of which I was inordinately proud when I came to mull over the match on the return trip to Calcutta. The first was against the off spinner who was bowling to a deep mid wicket and a long on; since I'm no Srikkanth, I rejected the possibility of clearing them so I skipped down the wicket (at least it felt as if I was skipping down the wicket), cleared the infield and dissected the two outfielders perfectly for four runs. At the other end Shastri was bowling more slowly to five men on the off side: unfortunately my flawed technique does not (appear to) allow me to hit left arm spinners on the leg side so I opted for a lofted extra cover drive, relying upon my natural inside out swing of the bat.

For me these shots have to be premeditated. I come down the wicket and if the ball is in the right place, the plan is executed. Problems obviously arise when the ball is in the wrong place, the early warning system fails and you carry on regardless. Anyway the admirably accurate Shastri bowled and I hit the ball for four to the nominated spot – very satisfying.

Thereafter runs came quickly and the need for extravagant risks diminished: we had seized the initiative and it was the bowlers who were now under pressure. Paul hit Shastri through the covers and began to unfurl his Knott-style sweep shots and we added 58 in 9 overs. Then for the second successive time I ran myself out hesitating foolishly over a second run to third man just when England had become firm favourites to win the match, Richard Ellison, a staunch one-day cricketer for Kent, now joined Downton as the light began to diminish along with India's over rate. On the players' balcony Tony Brown's and Stephanie Fowler's pocket calculators were now in constant use as it became clear that the light, or lack of it, would prevent the match lasting 49 overs. In the pressbox the journalists were scribbling away by torchlight as Downton rejected the umpires' offer to go off since we were still behind the required run rate. However with 20 runs needed from 4 overs even those without calculators realised that we were now in front of the rate and immediately twelfth man Chris Cowdrey was rushed out of the dressing room to sprint into the field with a pair of batting gloves for Paul. Paul, whose mathematics were equal to the situation, was a little embarrassed by Cowdrey's presence on the square. 'I don't want any gloves', he said as Cowdrey, with all the subtlety of Inspector Clouseau, whispered that he should now lodge an appeal against the light. The umpires, quite legitimately, decided that conditions had not deteriorated significantly since their previous offer; however whilst Amarnath bowled the 46th over, from which 9 runs accrued, the light worsened still further. Paul, whilst scrambling a second run yelled 'your end Elly – I think', only to be almost maimed himself by the return throw. Later Downton, the most objective of cricketers, described the light as the darkest he had ever experienced. The umpires led the players off the field with Downton and Ellison jubilant whilst the Indians, dejected by their defeat, did not complain about the decision.

So we had escaped defeat despite our lack-lustre performance of the morning and we were now 2–0 ahead in the five match series. The long haul back to Calcutta (two hours in a coach, one hour in the air) was perfectly tolerable – such irritants always are when you have won. There I celebrated with a few late night drinks in the bar before collapsing into my bed (I was very tired) eagerly awaiting the morning. My wife was arriving on the ten o'clock flight from Delhi.

EAST ZONE v ENGLAND XI

Played at Nehru Stadium, Gauhati. December 19, 20, 21
Toss: ENGLAND XI ENGLAND XI won by an innings and 121 runs

ENGLAND XI

G. Fowler	c sub (R. Bora) b Kumar	114
M. D. Moxon	c Jayaprakash b Doshi	36
A. J. Lamb	b Jayaprakash	23
*M. W. Gatting	c Arun Lal b Kumar	37
C. S. Cowdrey	st Deora by Jayaprakash	9
V. J. Marks	b Kumar	7
P. H. Edmonds	run out	6
P. R. Downton	c Dubey b Kumar	3
†B. N. French	c Deora b Doshi	13
N. A. Foster	not out	26
N. G. Cowans	c Bharadwaj b Kumar	1
Extras	(B5 LB5 W3 NB2)	15
Total		290

Fall of Wickets: 1–86, 2–119, 3–180, 4–193, 5–220, 6–243, 7–248, 8–251, 9–277, 10–290.
Bowling: Randhir Singh 8–1–19–0; Sinha 8–1–37–0; Doshi 37–6–90–2; Kumar 38.3–14–81–5; Jayaprakash 11–0–53–2.

EAST ZONE

K. Dubey	lbw b Foster	0	c Gatting b Foster	8
Arun Lal	b Marks	42	c Cowdrey b Foster	2
A Mitra	lbw b Edmonds	7	c Cowdrey b Foster	0
A. Jayaprakash	b Marks	16	lbw b Cowans	2
A. Bharadwaj	c and b Marks	0	b Marks	30
A. Das	c French b Marks	7	b Edmonds	3
†R. Deora	c French b Gatting	12	c Gatting b Edmonds	0
Randhir Singh	not out	9	run out	0
A. Sinha	c Gatting b Cowans	9	st French b Edmonds	0
*D. R. Doshi	c French b Cowans	4	b Edmonds	0
A. Kumar	b Edmonds	2	not out	6
Extras	(B4 LB4 W1)	9	(B1)	1
Total		117		52

Fall of Wickets:
1st Innings: 1–0, 2–26, 3–69, 4–69, 5–70, 6–83, 7–95, 8–106, 9–112, 10–117.
2nd Innings: 1–3, 2–3, 3–12, 4–14, 5–17, 6–27, 7–37, 8–38, 9–38, 10–52.
Bowling:
1st Innings: Foster 10–4–14–1; Cowans 9–2–18–2; Edmonds 33–16–25–2; Marks 29–11–48–4; Gatting 4–1–4–1.
2nd Innings: Foster 15–6–32–3; Cowans 6–3–4–1; Edmonds 9–3–13–4; Marks 0.4–0–2–1.
Umpires: M. Y. Gupte and V. K. Ramaswamy.

INDIA v ENGLAND (SECOND ONE-DAY INTERNATIONAL)

Played at Baribati Stadium, Cuttack. December 27

Toss: ENGLAND ENGLAND won on faster scoring rate

INDIA

*K. Srikkanth	lbw b Gatting	99
R. J. Shastri	b Gatting	102
D. B. Vengsarkar	c Gower b Marks	23
Yashpal Sharma	lbw b Marks	4
M. Armarnath	not out	1
R. M. H. Binny	b Marks	2
*S. M. Gavaskar	not out	6
†K. S. More		
M. Prabhakar	did not bat	
R. S. Ghai		
A. Patel		
Extras	(B5 LB5 W3 NB2)	15
Total	(5 wkts 49 Overs)	252

Fall of Wickets: 1–188, 2–235, 3–243, 4–243, 5–246.

Bowling: Foster 5–0–26–0; Cowans 10–0–39–0; Ellison 6–0–31–0; Edmonds 10–0–47–0; Marks 8–0–50–3; Gatting 10–0–49–2.

ENGLAND

G. Fowler	c Vengsarkar b Binny	15
R. T. Robinson	b Prabhakar	1
M. W. Gatting	b Patel	59
*D. I. Gower	c Prabhakar b Binny	21
A. J. Lamb	run out	28
V. J. Marks	run out	44
†P. R. Downton	not out	44
R. M. Ellison	not out	14
P. H. Edmonds		
N. A. Foster	did not bat	
N. G. Cowans		
Extras	(LB9 W1 NB5)	15
Total	(6 wkts 46 Overs)	241

Fall of Wickets: 1–3, 2–50, 3–93, 4–128, 5–145, 6–203.

Bowling: Ghai 8–0–40–0; Prabhakar 10–1–34–1; Binny 7–0–48–2; Patel 10–0–53–1; Shastri 10–0–48–0; Amarnath 1–0–9–0.

Umpires: J. D. Ghosh and P. G. Pandit.

9
Calcutta

Lord Hawke probably took the same view as I do about families on tour with the MCC players – it is no more a place for them than a trench on the Somme. Thus wrote John Woodcock after England's ill-fated tour to Australia in 1974/75. Apparently England's pace attack were scampering around the hotel dining room desperately trying to force cornflakes down their offsprings' throats on the morning of a Test match.

Whatever the rights and wrongs of that situation, I felt that it was essential for my wife, Anna, and myself that she came to India. Playing cricket for a living, with all its obvious attractions and glamour, puts an enormous strain upon personal relationships and marriages. Constant separation both at home in the summer and during winter tours inevitably takes its toll and it surprises me that the TCCB does not help finance our wives' travelling expenses as any other overseas employer would. I can hear a few traditionalists muttering that thirty years ago we travelled by boat to Australia, the trip took six months and the wives stayed at home, where they belonged. Well, the frequency of tours has increased since then, women's role in society has changed and also it is worth examining how many broken marriages have arisen amongst the cricketing fraternity during that period. 'Is another cricket tour worth a broken marriage?' It is a distasteful question but it occasionally arises.

My wife reliably informs me that it's no fun being a cricket widow. Who gets the car serviced, walks the dog, changes the fuses, pays the bills, tends the garden, buys the Christmas tree and hides her face in the shops when Matthew Engel has reported another batting failure by Marks? She does, not to mention the washing up. So she organises a trip to India and to cap it all has to spend two days at the Calcutta Test at Eden Gardens, a spectacle that could not possibly match watching 'Come Dancing' in a deserted Tiverton living room in the middle of December. More, though not much more, on the Third Test in a moment.

To visit Calcutta first on a trip to India is like starting an English Literature course with James Joyce. Initially it is a trifle intimidating. When I met Anna at the airport, we were immediately submerged by taxi drivers seeking our custom and as we were driven towards the city at alarming speed, we were overcome by the stench of the lakes in the suburbs and the waste tips where paupers rummaged for tins and bottles and any other saleable commodities. Entering the city, we passed by the hovels, whose numbers and squalor outmatch anything we'd seen before. Semi-clothed children mingled with hogs and goats along the side of the streets and when we finally reached our hotel, we were greeted by a disarmingly cheerful beggar, hunch-backed with mutilated arms, a massive boil on his cheek and a toothy Colgate-free grin. He was ever present in Chowringee Road, often frantically waving directions to our coach driver before asking for rupees and yet not in the least disconsolate if he didn't receive any. Anna was relieved to withdraw to the safety of our hotel, whilst I pretended to be battle-hardened. However within several hours my intrepid wife was urging me out to discover some of the sights of Calcutta.

Over the next few days we were grateful for the enlightened approach of the management who allowed me to disappear from Eden Gardens for two days (I wasn't playing again). Already David Gower and Tim Robinson have escaped to Rajasthan. Bruch French, the mountaineer, flew north to the Himalayas to inspect Everest, maybe to contemplate a future conquest, and after the Third Test Allan Lamb and his wife went to Fisherman's Cove, south of Madras, for four days by the beach. Such interludes away from our sheltered existence in hotels are always worthwhile even if they are not possible for every member of the party.

So during our stay we glimpsed some of the contrasts of Calcutta – the remnants of the Raj at the Tollygunge Club, now famous for Boycott's last day as an England player. In a way, you can't blame him for sneaking off there. The greens are excellent and there's always the prospect of a drink even on dry days thanks to the generous hospitality of Bob Wright, the secretary, who still manages to live in the style of many Englishmen in Calcutta between the wars. There is also the stately Victoria Memorial Building, regarded now as an unhappy attempt by the British to build a better Taj Mahal, from whose walls grim governor generals peer down like austere public school headmasters and alongside the Hooghly river is the Governor General's extensive country residence, now deserted except for a few loitering vultures and the massive, forlorn statues of King George VI. The great helicopter fans are static now, maybe the punkah wallahs are dragging rickshaws around Calcutta's narrow streets.

On a fog-ridden, smog-ridden boat trip with the Fowlers and the Pococks we visited a shrine of Mahatma Gandhi. We all removed our shoes out of respect for Indian custom and also to allow the sacred water of the Hooghly to wash our feet, despite a dog's carcase floating down the river twenty yards away. There we examined a frieze of Gandhi's life and noted the awe in the voices of our guides as they described the scenes depicted. I don't suppose Gandhi spent much time at the Tollygunge Club. After a few days Anna was totally fearless so we strode through some of the darker areas of Calcutta to visit the Kali temple. Unlike most tourist attractions this temple was very much alive and crowded with Indians practising their religion. We imagined that it was in this sort of place in Jerusalem that Jesus overturned the tables as we saw artisans and moneychangers mingling with the worshippers around the perimeter of this tiny shrine. Fortunately as we approached the temple, a priest (so he said) had spotted our white faces and wide eyes and had led us down a dark alleyway to the entrance. He informed us of the daily sacrifices of a goat to the goddess, which fresh bloodstains confirmed. The meat would then be cooked and distributed to the beggars that flock around the shrine. He demanded rupees, not for himself (of course) but for the destitute and we handed them over without argument nor complete confidence about their destination.

We also decided to inspect Calcutta's Botanical Gardens and in particular the 200 year old Banyan tree, which is claimed to be the largest in the world, covering an area of 400 metres in circumference and still flourishing despite having its central trunk removed in 1925 due to fungus damage. The scheduled twenty minute drive took almost two hours as we bumped into an election parade celebrating the Congress Party's victory. As we crawled through the congested streets of the Howrah district of Calcutta our taxi driver lived up to the reputation of the Bengali, emotional, argumentative, yet eager to please – some of our finest hospitality came from this derelict city. For years Calcutta had been the Marxist stronghold of India, but in the December election the Congress Party of Rajiv Gandhi had captured half the seats. Throughout the rest of the country, however, Mr Gandhi won by Thatcher, nay Reagan proportions. For weeks every available piece of stonework had been meticulously decorated by the motifs of the major parties. The open hand of the Congress Party, and the Lotus Flower of the Janata Party and in Calcutta, the hammer and sickle. There were obviously firm unwritten laws that these emblems should not be obliterated by the opposition, instead we read a neat inscription 'Stamp on this Sign', which suggested that a certain pre-school morality still pervades Indian politics; however a few cocktail party political commentators assured me that such innocence may not stretch to the higher echelons of Indian political life. The Congress Party distributed millions of posters and I estimate about 70% were of Indira Gandhi, 30% of Rajiv. The pundits claimed that Rajiv was eager to call an election swiftly to demonstrate to the world that India was back to normal after the assassination, yet he must also have been anxious to exploit the sympathy vote, it was Rajiv's Falklands factor. The cynics suggested that Mrs Gandhi won the election far more convincingly dead that she would have done alive. All of which mattered very little to the jubilant throng at Howrah who were beating their drums, waving their flags, and applauding some distant microphone as the two of us huddled together in the back seat of our taxi wondering why we wanted to look at a blessed Banyan tree in the first place. Nevertheless by Indian standards we learnt that the election had been conducted in a peaceful, straightforward manner.

However, the politics of Indian Cricket had become far from straightforward. The dropping of Kapil for the Third Test is akin to the BBC axing the Morecambe and Wise Christmas show in the seventies. It prompted leader articles in the national papers and at Eden Gardens the entrance gate was daubed with 'No Kapil, No Test', a threat which the Bengali passion for cricket would never allow to be fulfilled. The Indian selectors announced that he had been dropped for disciplinary reasons and they gave this version of events in the Indian dressing room on the fifth day of the Delhi Test. Two of the selectors, Amber Roy and Kripal Singh, witnessed an exchange between Kapil Dev and Gavaskar during the final afternoon. Kapil reportedly claimed 'The match is safe. I'm going to have a slog'. Gavaskar disagreed: 'We're only 100 ahead. It won't be safe until an hour after tea. Play your normal game'. Kapil then apparently said casually 'slogging is my normal game'. There were also suggestions that Kapil had undermined Gavaskar's authority at Bombay by surreptitiously rearranging the field after Sunil had set it.

Maybe the egoes of both players prevent either from playing whole-heartedly for the other and the traditional regional rivalries between Bombay and the North can only have exacerbated the situation. With India's astonishing World Cup victory under Kapil's leadership, Sunil's authority was completely undermined. True, he played under Kapil's captaincy but with a recklessness and abandon that Fletcher's tourists would never have recognised. At Calcutta against the West Indies, Gavaskar was pilloried by the crowd as he slashed wildly at two successive deliveries from Michael Holding when India were struggling to avoid an innings defeat; the first was dropped, the second caught by the wicketkeeper. However he escaped the axe and at Madras scored a memorable, aggressive 200. Had he changed his approach to batting because to attack was the best way to survive against the West Indies or did this policy suggest that the iron commitment of the seventies was beginning to wane?

However, I regarded Kapil's omission not as evidence of a petty personal vendetta but as a short, sharp, shock treatment designed to shake India's top all-rounder back to his peak for the Fourth Test on the assumption that the placid Eden Gardens wicket would eventually ensure a draw. This assessment stems from my limited experience of Sunil, which has been entirely favourable. At Somerset in 1980 he was a delight, devoid of any of the trappings of an international superstar and always co-operative even though he had to endure playing under my captaincy on several occasions. Botham nicknamed him 'Swoop' because of his stark refusal to dive in the field under any circumstances and guffawed at his Achilles heel, his fear of dogs, which prompted Somerset's (present) captain to introduce them into the dressing room at every opportunity. We all enjoyed his mischievous, self-effacing sense of humour and after three months we still wondered where he hid that hard streak of ruthlessness that had brought him 8000 Test runs, into dispute with the Indian authorities on several occasions, and which prompted him to treat a one-day international against England as batting practice. It never surfaced at Taunton and we loved him. Maybe the simple countrymen from the West are too naive for I'm bound to say that Kapil Dev has never struck me as a Genghis Khan figure either.

Anyway, at Calcutta we expected the decision to be rescinded with the introduction into the saga of Mr N. K. P. Salve, the President of the Board of Control for Cricket in India and a cabinet minister – until Rajiv's reshuffle. A week before the election Salve sent a telegram to a Mr Priya Ranjan Das Mushi, a Congress candidate in the north offering the services of Congress I's latest recruit, Kapil Dev. I presume this had nothing to do with the cricketing manoeuvres of the time, yet I'd never previously regarded Kapil as a political animal. Next Salve summoned both Gavaskar and Kapil to Nagpur for a reconciliation, which at least gave credence to the story that there had been an altercation in the first place. Clearly Salve was anxious that his latest political prodigy should be restored to the Indian side and the next we hear, the selectors are meeting to consider the possibility of adding a 15th man to the Test squad. 'Whoever can the 15th man be?'

We all mused without a trace of curiosity. This meeting lasted seven hours and at the end the selectors (as a body) unanimously declared that Kapil would not be reinstated. The conclusion of the meeting was delayed by the need to phone Salve to discover whether the addition of a 15th man was a directive or merely a suggestion. If it was a directive, then all sorts of possibilities arose such as the resignation of the Selection Committee or perhaps, Gavaskar himself because of this outside interference. They learnt that it was a suggestion. If there is a moral here for Neil McFarlane, Mrs Thatcher's Minister of Sport, I suppose it is 'leave P. B. H. May to his own devices'.

So to our surprise and relief India took to the field without their most charismatic cricketer. No doubt Kapil, who by now had admitted that his dismissal at Delhi was a trifle foolhardy, was disappointed yet at least he was spared the tedium of one of the dreariest Tests in recent history. It irks me to have to try to describe it – so maybe I won't. Obviously anyone who has reached this point in my jottings is a person of high intelligence and vivid imagination. Now is the time to use it. Look at the score card and picture a massive concrete bowl packed with 75,000 people as Calcutta's early morning smog finally yields to the sun and piece it together yourself. I'll anticipate a few of your queries.

'Who is Azharuddin?' He is a 22 year old from Hyberabad who scored 150 against us in that disastrous game at Ahmedabad. He was preferred to Srikanth in this match and judging by the neat, assured manner in which he scored a century he will play for India for years to come. The more we see of him, the higher we rate him, which is an ominous sign. He is a deft, wristy batsman, especially strong off the back foot and through the onside. Off the field he is quiet, unassuming and entirely unaffected by his success.

'Why were only two innings completed in five days?' It rained on New Year's Day for the first time in 28 years in Calcutta and only four overs were bowled. Anna and I went to the races and met up with Donald Carr, the Secretary of the TCCB, who appeared to have as much chance of picking a winner as Arthur Scargill has of editing *The Daily Telegraph*. Moreover India batted very slowly, Shastri being the main culprit; in the newspapers he openly admitted that the prospect of a century ruled out any thoughts of being more adventurous. The Indians seem to attach far more importance to such individual landmarks than any of us would care to admit. One disillusioned English journalist described his hundred as 'a pot-hunt, an innings played without regard for the match or the crowd who paid to watch it'.

'Why did Gower bowl three overs in the Indian first innings?' (I trust you spotted that.) As the Indian innings meandered into the fourth afternoon, Gower finally lodged his own silent protest – very mild in comparison to the hoots of fury and derision from the crowd – at Gavaskar's decision to keep batting, by bowling what may politely be described as off-breaks. Meanwhile Edmonds, never one to miss an opportunity for the bizarre, peered at a newspaper in Warwick Armstrong style.

Gavaskar was universally chastised for not declaring earlier and thereby ruining the match; however the placid nature of the Eden Gardens pitch and the loss of the second day made a draw inevitable whenever he declared.

'If the pitch was so good, why were England all out for 276?' The Englishmen are not such avid pothunters. Once the Test was obviously safe our concentration lapsed. Mike Gatting, however, maintained his dominance over Siva, hitting him for five fours in as many overs during his 45 minute innings of 48. The little leg spinner is looking less effective and less confident every match; at the crease Gatting adopts the demeanour of an irate school bully, whom Siva increasingly wants to avoid at all costs. The match ended in farce as Allan Lamb, who had been wooing the crowd by stealing a policeman's helmet and lathi as he patrolled the third man boundary, took his first Test wicket trapping Prabhakar lbw. He celebrated with exaggerated glee and afterwards reflected that the unfortunate Indian opening bowler, though out, was nowhere near as plumb as Allan Border at Perth in 1982.

'Were Gower and the side disappointed by the outcome?' Disappointed by the desultory nature of the game but not by our performance in the field. John Woodcock of *The Times*, who had just arrived in India, commented on the excellence of the fielding, which he said was a sure sign of a buoyant team spirit which may sound an old-fashioned assessment (reminiscent of my Oxford days: 'We may be outbowled and outbatted, but, by golly we'll surpass them in the field') but it is nonetheless accurate.

Our bowlers, too, verged on the heroic; if you look at the bowling figures you'll notice that even 'Flash' Cowans yielded no more than two and a half runs per over. Norman's bowling has definitely developed on this tour and crucially so has his confidence. It is ironic that England's fastest bowlers (Cowans and Dilley) are mild gentle men who need to be bolstered up rather than simply having any innate aggression channelled in the right direction. I have never heard Norman utter a word to an opposition batsman, whereas medium pacer Paul Allott, for instance, is not averse to unleashing a formidable stream of invective. I'm not suggesting that Flash should launch a fierce verbal assault towards Gavaskar, but if he were to say anything it would reflect a welcome rise in his (own) self-esteem.

Imperceptibly Richard Ellison has also grown in confidence. I mentioned back in Sri Lanka that his slow, ponderous drawl made him a figure of fun, yet by Christmas this side of his personality was never focused upon – initially he allowed himself to appear slow-witted as a defence mechanism, a disguise to hide behind, yet now his opinion at team meetings, for instance, is often sought after and respected and in his own right he has become one of the characters of the touring party. At Calcutta we marvelled at his competitiveness: even in his 50th over he was still swinging the ball away, occasionally beating the bat and as he plodded back to his mark, revealing a wry, wistful smile. To bowl 50 overs without taking a wicket is extremely frustrating (I know, I've done it) and yet Elly kept bounding in ever-hopeful.

Both spinners were miserly in their different styles. Pat Pocock, tossing one up in the air, skidding a faster one, wide of the crease, an arm ball, cannot resist seeking endless variations. Occasionally this approach misfires if his rhythm is awry at the beginning of the spell. Most spinners simply aim for maidens in their first over but I think 'Percy' aims for wicket maidens. Paul Downton is in an excellent position to compare him to John Emburey: 'John is a pressure bowler, whose first objective is to tie his man down, trap him and then force him into error, whilst Pat is always seeking a straightforward and immediate deception'. Maybe Percy is simply being true to his character. Despite his 38 years he retains the exuberance of an excitable schoolboy. If there are juvenile pranks Pocock along with his new side kick Fowler are prime suspects. He has a restless inventive mind quick to analyse and theorise about cricket. Derek Underwood has self-deprecatingly described himself as a 'low mentality bowler'. Percy will never be that. He is also a marvellous room mate though I've yet to have that pleasure. For ten years at Surrey he partnered Jackman and they became great friends. However their evenings often followed different patterns. Jackers in his prime required a little sleep and a lot of alcohol whilst Percy disliked having his night disturbed by the sounds of Jackman grovelling for the light switch, bumping into furniture and chasing his toothpaste around the bathroom. So every night Percy left the bathroom light on, moved every piece of furniture out of Jackers' slipway and squeezed the toothpaste onto the Jackman toothbrush to assist his arrival and Percy slept soundly ever after.

Phil Edmonds, however, was our most successful bowler at Calcutta. It is remarkable having played Test Cricket only sporadically over the last five years that within two weeks of this tour everyone regarded him as the crucial member of the bowling attack and no doubt Henri agreed with this assessment. Up until now his career must have been extremely frustrating for he could have represented England sixty times but for a personality clash with Brearley and mistrust from Willis. In the past I suppose that his intellect, his physical presence and his considerable self-belief may have posed a threat to his captain. However, these qualities do not seem to threaten Gower and why should they? It is Gower who has brought him back from the wilderness and if Henri doesn't perform it is his career, not Gower's, that is finally doomed. No doubt behind the self-confident exterior there lurks some insecurity, which might be reflected in the stutter in his run up and his occasionally fierce reaction to criticism. Yet on this tour he has also been prepared to chuckle at himself especially when acquiescing in a team discussion – 'Of course you're absolutely right, forgive me for speaking'. Everyone knows that such statements lack complete conviction and that he is parodying the reformed troublemaker and yet it marks a concession on his part. He has been a success on the field as well, bowling with superb control. In contrast to Pocock he doesn't aim for much variety – simply to bowl the unplayable ball every time he runs up to the wicket, it should pitch on middle-leg and just clip the off bail. Of course that doesn't happen very often but it remains his goal and it results in great accuracy.

So the Calcutta Test did us no harm. Of the two captains (both short of runs) the pressure is still very much upon Gavaskar, who was vigorously pilloried by the crowd and in the press for the delayed declaration and the dropping of Kapil. In fact Sunil declared that he would never play for India in Calcutta again (so did Pat Pocock but no one seemed to pay much attention to that) and England still maintained the psychological ascendancy gained in Delhi but it was a dreadful match.

A much more exciting game was played at Salt Lake City, ten miles outside of Calcutta, at an orphanage, where two sides, led by Foster and Marks contested an animated 15 overs match. Our teams were comprised of the cricket enthusiasts of this SOS village, which was made known to us by Scyld Berry, who in turn had been introduced by Mike Brearley. Neil Foster was an immediate success with the children. Before his side took to the field he summoned his mystified troops into a circle to carry out Bernard Thomas's stretching exercises and all the while he encouraged them in that broad Essex country dialect, which by comparison makes Keith Fletcher appear to speak with a plum in his mouth. His charges didn't understand much, but it didn't matter. The wicket might be charitably described as sporting. The opening bowlers, fired by the presence of such important guests, charged in like raging Bengali tigers against batsmen protected by one flimsy pad and a pair of makeshift batting gloves. My first two batsmen were caught off vicious lifters so I hastily rearranged the batting order so that I should tackle the more trustworthy spinners of Foster and Berry. Indeed I edged the innings towards respectability with a doughty knock before succumbing to the guiles of Berry's wrist-spin, his first Test wicket.

When my side fielded the excitable nature of the Bengalis came to the fore. One batsman gloved the ball to the wicketkeeper yet after numerous vociferous appeals he was given not out. The umpire (one of the dismissed batsmen) was immediately surrounded by the entire side and a potential riot situation emerged. No one responded to my 'Come on, chaps, let's get on with the game' – I presume their English was minimal – and I was on the point of abdication when the furore subsided as quickly as it arose. Finally the opposition needed two to win off the last ball, whereupon Foster, the cad, hit a boundary. Everyone had so obviously enjoyed the afternoon that it was a real pleasure to be there. After the match we were surrounded by the orphans and bombarded with questions and we could not avoid being moved by the warmth and enthusiasm of our welcome. Later we had tea with the father of the village and learnt a little about it.

The SOS movement began in post-war Austria as a dream of one Dr Hermann Gmeiner to help the refugee children of war-torn Europe and the first village was founded in 1949. The movement aims to fulfil three needs: (1) care of the unwanted child in a family set up; (2) an occupation as Mother for the needy woman dedicated to social work; (3) direct participation in social work for a large number of people through the sponsorship programme. In India the first village was established near Delhi in 1964 and there are now 21 throughout the country. The village at Salt Lake City comprises twenty houses and was completed in 1977, now 200 children live and grow in a cluster of family houses, each in the independent care of an SOS mother as the household head.

The children share the surname of the mother and the village itself functions like a joint family under the village father; each family consists of approximately ten children of varying ages, who attend the local schools thereby encouraging integration with the local community.

The village father, Mr Mitra, a saintly man, took us around some of the houses and proudly introduced us to some of the smiling faces, reciting the name and background of each child that we met. Few spoke English, but again it didn't matter. We left uplifted by our visit, having witnessed a sure sign of hope amidst the desperate poverty of much of Calcutta. Indeed, I'll remember our epic 15 over match far more vividly than anything that happened at Eden Gardens.

INDIA v ENGLAND (THIRD TEST MATCH)

Played at Eden Gardens, Calcutta. December 31, January 1, 3, 4, 5
Toss: INDIA Match Drawn

INDIA

Batsman	1st Innings		2nd Innings	
*S. M. Gavaskar	c Gatting b Edmonds	13		
A. D. Gaekwad	c Downton b Cowans	18		
D. B. Vengsarkar	b Edmonds	48		
M. Amarnath	c Cowdrey b Edmonds	42		
M. Azharuddin	c Gower b Cowans	110		
R. J. Shastri	b Cowans	111	(1) not out	7
†S. M. H. Kirmani	c Fowler b Pocock	35		
M. Prabhakar	not out	35	(2) lbw b Lamb	21
C. Sharma	not out	13		
N. S. Yadav	did not bat		(3) not out	0
L. Sivaramakrishnan				
Extras	(LB8 W1 NB3)	12	(NB1)	1
Total	(7 wkts dec)	437	(1 wkt)	29

Fall of Wickets:
1st Innings: 1–28, 2–35, 3–126, 4–127, 5–341, 6–356, 7–407.
2nd Innings: 1–29.

Bowling:
1st Innings: Cowans 41–12–103–3; Ellison 53–14–117–0; Edmonds 47–22–72–3; Pocock 52–14–108–1; Gatting 2–1–1–0; Cowdrey 2–0–15–0; Gower 3–0–13–0.
2nd Innings: Cowans 4–1–6–0; Ellison 1–0–1–0; Cowdrey 4–0–10–0; Edmonds 4–3–2–0; Pocock 2–1–4–0; Fowler 1–1–0–0; Robinson 1–1–0–0; Lamb 1–0–6–1.

ENGLAND

Batsman	1st Innings	
G. Fowler	c Vengsarkar b Sivaramakrishnan	49
R. T. Robinson	b Yadav	36
*D. I. Gower	c Shastri b Yadav	19
P. I. Pocock	c Azharuddin b Sivaramakrishnan	5
M. W. Gatting	b Yadav	48
A. J. Lamb	c Kirmani b Sharma	67
C. S. Cowdrey	lbw b Yadav	27
†P. R. Downton	not out	6
P. H. Edmonds	c Gavaskar b Sharma	8
R. M. Ellison	c and b Sharma	1
N. G. Cowans	b Sharma	1
Extras	(LB2 NB7)	9
Total		276

Fall of Wickets: 1–71, 2–98, 3–110, 4–162, 5–163, 6–229, 7–269, 8–270, 9–273.
Bowling: Sharma 12.3–0–38–4; Prabhakar 5–1–16–0; Sivaramakrishnan 28–7–90–2; Yadav 32–10–86–4; Shastri 23–6–44–0.
Umpires: B. Ganguli and V. Raju.

10
Hyderabad

At Hyderabad there was a lake which bordered the gardens of an hotel. Upon it sat four cumbersome barges and forty yards from the shore there was a floating fountain which was floodlit by night. Now there was not a great deal to do in the evenings in Hyderabad except to entertain our wives and sweethearts, who now numbered seven – their presence certainly added sparkle to our cocktail parties. So the gauntlet was thrown down by Chris Lander of the *Daily Mirror* for a floodlit boat race between press and players. Clearly such a challenge could not be refused and stakes were arranged and a course from the shore, twice around the fountain, back to the shore again, was established for this epic contest.

Each barge was to be propelled by two oarsmen. The press were represented by Lander and Colin Bateman (*Daily Express*) and Graham Otway (Press Association) and Peter Baxter (BBC), the players by Gower and French, Cowdrey and Gatting. I was amazed by the arrogance – or naivety – of the press's challenge for our men seemed invincible even before the race began. For Gower, as England's captain, is well versed in steering a leaky ship, and his partner French is universally regarded as intrepid and fearless since he climbs mountains, whilst Cowdrey and Gatting are the two avid game players in the party, who are loathe to lose at anything. At 9.30 p.m. the crews arrived at the shore wearing the nearest that they could muster to waterproofs and the race began. Even though the outcome was entirely predictable, the contest was not without incident: the barges had no obvious means of steering so collisions were inevitable; they would have been anyway. Cowdrey and Gatting in their eagerness to cut corners became jammed under the fountain and were completely drenched whilst the press soon became entangled with one another. Meanwhile our captain calmly guided his boat to victory despite the onset of missiles (oranges) from the eighth floor room of a giggling Lancastrian and a superannuated Londoner. Later I mentioned to Allan Lamb that it had reminded me of the Battle of Salamis and he nodded blankly.

This highly successful entertainment highlights the fact that the press, whether we like it or not, are an integral part of our tour. They share the same planes, the same hotels, the same bars and restaurants and we are in constant communion with them. So armed with my tape machine I decided to turn the tables and interview one of them. I chose Peter Smith of the *Daily Mail*, partly because I knew he wouldn't refuse and partly because after John Woodcock, who has just arrived in India, he is the most experienced journalist on the tour. I thought I'd begin with a really penetrating question.

VM: When did you first tour with England?

PS: In 1965/66 on Mike Smith's tour to Australia writing for the *Daily Sketch*. I also acted as cover for Crawford White of the *Express* so that he could have some time off. When the MCC went to New Zealand for the last four weeks of the tour, the established writers returned home and I stayed on working for the *Standard*, the *Daily Herald*, *Daily Mail*, *The People*, *News of the World*, anyone who wanted me. I toured for the next three years; then the *Sketch* folded and there was a lull of five years. This trip is my thirteenth overseas tour.

VM: I find it incredible after twelve tours that you still appear to enjoy the lifestyle and the cricket. How do you manage it?

PS: I've always enjoyed watching cricket and I enjoy meeting new people each time. Even though the centres we visit are often the same, I'm surrounded by new personalities and I like watching them develop as cricketers and as people.

VM: And new journalists as well?

PS: Yes, I see more of my colleagues than my wife. Like you, we are separated for 4½ months in the winter, but at least you are guaranteed half of your matches in an English season at home whereas I have to go to where the story is. I suppose my wife and I don't have much time to get fed up with one another.

VM: You are chairman of the Cricket Writers Society and also the press 'spokesman' over here. How did this come about?

PS: It happened by accident. In the past on tour both press and players used the same travel agents and the same hotels yet as independent groups. Eventually the TCCB said to the press 'let's make up one large group' – for economic reasons. But in practice it didn't work too well: the press would be marooned in airport lounges whilst the players disappeared in their luxury coaches. In the West Indies in 1980 we arrived in Antigua to a rum punch celebration in the VIP lounge: a local West Indian collected all the players' passports and within minutes they were returned all stamped and the players departed for the hotel whilst the press were just left there. Everyone started complaining that we had to go through customs whilst the players had walked straight through. There was much mumbling along the lines of having a strong word with Peter Lush at the TCCB when we returned but that would have done nothing for us in the West Indies. So I decided to go to the manager, A. C. Smith and I asked him 'What time is the baggage leaving?', he replied '*Our* baggage is at 9 o'clock. I don't know about yours'. I said 'We're all in the same group as one big party: if your baggage is 9 o'clock, then so is ours'. Eventually both sets of baggage disappeared at 9 o'clock and from that moment I was designated as the man who talked to AC and it all stemmed from there. So now I liaise with the locals on behalf of the press about air tickets, press tickets and telex operators and also if the press as a group want some information from Tony Brown, I'll be the one who asks.

VM: Do you have a special role in England as well?

PS: Again, it's a liaison role. I work more closely with PBH (May) than my colleagues. PBH does not like phone calls. We learn the Test team early on Sunday morning and PBH is only available between the hours of 9 am and 10 am, when at least a dozen reporters would want to ask him for comment upon the selection. So a system has developed whereby I'll phone PBH at 9 am and spend half an hour with him and anyone else who can't get through will phone me.

VM: What are the particular problems of a cricket journalist touring India.

PS: The telex facilities can be a constant nightmare. On Test match days there are usually adequate facilities but the Indians don't realise that we have to send previews on the day before and we can spend six or seven hours in a telex office before our copy gets through. One example from the last tour. We went to Jammu, up in the north, and there were no telex facilities in sight on the day before the match. We spoke to the local telex chief who said 'Don't worry we will have four machines for you at the ground'. We go to the match the next morning and there's nothing – just one Sikh sitting at a desk raised behind the press box. Graham Otway asked 'Where are the four machines!' 'Don't worry Sir, we have four machines.' Otway persisted, 'You say you've got four machines. I'd like to see them please' – 'Yes we have four – two men and two bicycles'.

You can never relax during a match unless you are sure your telex is going out.

VM: Are your sports editors always aware of these problems?

PS: Often they're not as they have been deskbound since their early days.

VM: Can you describe one day as a cricket journalist – let's say the first day of a Test match.

PS: We always arrive early to establish our positions in the press box. Seats are rarely allocated as in England so we often have to turf out the wives and kids of local officials. One problem here is that the Indians being on the small side, in contrast to some of the English press corps, are used to working in cramped conditions. On a row of desks where we might seat five, they seat ten so we have to establish our territorial rights at the start. Sometimes our view will be obscured by the sightscreen so we try to change that, usually in vain.

For the Agency men like Graham Otway, who is sending constant reports, it's important to find out the team announcements but the 'dailies' won't start writing until the close of play. Although there's a 5½ hour time advantage, we always start writing immediately the game has finished because we need that time to cope with the vagaries of the telex system.

We'll make detailed notes about the fall of wickets and any memorable moments.

VM: At what stage will you start to consider the day's angle – before the close of play?

PS: Usually yes. For instance, if England are batting and Foxy scores a century by ten, that will be the day's story and we'll begin to shape the day's play around him. In that situation we would dread a dramatic collapse in the last half-hour.

VM: Does this apply to writers of *The Times* as well as the *Sun*?

PS: You need to have a theme running through the piece, usually focusing on one person. John Woodcock and Mike Carey will probably start writing earlier than the rest of us since after their first 250 words they write a straightforward narrative of the day's play. The tabloids don't have the space for such detail. But every journalist aims to catch the mood of the day in his opening paragraphs.

VM: Where do you write the piece?

PS: I type it at the ground.

VM: How long does it take?

PS: Once I have the intro right in my mind, not long. I might spend half an hour agonising over the first three paragraphs and the next fifteen will flow swiftly. Everything hinges upon the introduction and usually at a Test match the writers will concentrate upon the same theme unless it has been a very nondescript 210–4 type day with no-one outstanding.

Once it's typed, I hand it to the telex man and spend most of the evening awaiting a phone call to confirm its safe arrival in London. I can't relax until I've received that call, which might say 'copy received', 'copy received by garbled' or 'where the hell is your copy?'

VM: How much advice or interference do you receive from your Sports Editor. Does it decrease the more experienced you are?

PS: Not necessarily. For instance in Delhi when I described the Second Test victory I began through the eyes of David Gower – something like 'David Gower was jubilant after England's first success under his captaincy but stressed the importance of maintaining this improvement in Calcutta . . .' Then five paragraphs later I said what a superb win it was for me as an Englishman in the stands, an overseas test victory has been an extraordinarily rare event in my experience. At 8 o'clock that night my boss phoned up and said 'You were pretty excited by that, weren't you?' 'Yes, I was.' 'Right', he said, 'I want that, I want you, Peter Smith, to write this piece and let your feelings show'. So I rewrote the first five paragraphs and I think that they were an improvement.

Another example was at Christchurch last year when we lost by an innings to New Zealand. Again he phoned and asked what I really thought of England's performance. I replied that it was bad and he wanted me to say so strongly. So I strengthened my piece. However my boss will never alter anything of mine without consulting me and in that sense I'm fortunate in comparison to some of my colleagues. Obviously those in the office, anxious to sell newspapers, are looking for extremes but he won't interfere without my agreement. Some papers will seize a headline from your copy at the merest hint of controversy and therefore distort the facts.

VM: Like the *Sun*'s 'Bottle Barrage Fury – England in Riot Terror' headline after the one-day game at Poona?

PS: Yes, that was a very minor incident. Fourth division stuff.

VM: You are now a very experienced tourist; can you compare the relationships between players and press now with when you started?

PS: It's not that different. The first time I was aware of any difficulties was on my first tour in 1956/66. Mike Smith was an extremely popular captain with both players and press and we all mixed happily together as we have on this tour. But when the cricket starts to go badly extra pressure arises. I can remember the rest day of the Adelaide Test: England were one up in the series having won at Sydney but on the third day at Adelaide we were dreadful. We were all relaxing by the pool and then one of the players bought an evening paper, which contained the quotebacks of our pieces of the previous day, under the screaming headline 'Pom Press Pummels England Players'. He sat reading the paper, and passed it to the next one and on to the next and gradually they all disappeared. After half an hour the group of fifteen (nine players and six pressmen) was reduced to the six pressmen, who were desperate to get hold of the paper and find out what the problem was.

VM: So nothing has changed?

PS: The only difference is that within two days it was all forgotten. Over the last three years the grudges have tended to linger longer than that.

VM: So would you say that modern players are more sensitive to criticism?

PS: Yes, they are – possibly because the pressures are far greater now. A tour was much more relaxed twenty years ago with a plethora of state matches and up-country games. Now we lurch from one-day international to Test match with little respite in between.

VM: Are you under increasing pressure from your sports editor to dig up some sort of controversy?

PS: I don't think so. Before I started touring there was a formidable gang of four, Crawford White of the *Express*, Brian Chapman of the *Mirror*, Charles Bray of the *Chronicle* and Lyn Wellings of the *Evening News* and they could be fairly vicious. There was a greater tendency to look for off-the-field stories. Now there are many more news stories – 'Are we going to SA or the West Indies?' 'Will the tour of India continue', etc. . . There are also many more previews as the tours become more condensed. So there was greater pressure to liven things up twenty years ago. In 1965/66 John Clark of the *Evening Standard* did a half-term report on each player. He wrote of one English all-rounder, 'If he played half as well on the field as he did off it, he'd be having a successful tour'. Some journalists used to sit up in the hotel lobby at midnight counting the players back in.

VM: That's a view that would surprise many modern cricketers especially in the light of last winter's tour.

PS: As you know, those off-the-field stories didn't stem from the cricket correspondents and even then our relationship didn't break down completely. This was probably helped by the fact that we were on our way to Faisalabad when the story in *The Mail on Sunday* broke. In such a remote backwater players and press inevitably had to dine in the same room of the Chenab Club. I can always remember the look of disbelief on A. C. Smith's face when some of the players actually came over to talk to the press.

VM: No doubt you've made good friends with players on tour. You've spent several hours in the bar with many of us, myself included. Are there any guidelines that you impose upon yourself as to what information you'll use.

PS: Any conversation that I have with an official or player over a drink, I will not repeat without permission. Reg Hayter taught me this years ago. Whenever I went to a sporting function Reg always insisted that I should be the last out of the bar. 'If people are going to talk, they'll do it when they've had a few to drink so go to the bar and stay there but if you dare use any of that you'll never work for me again. You phone the next morning and ask for permission to use what you've learnt.' That's what I told Graham Otway when he first joined us.

VM: Do friendships with a player affect how you write about them?

PS: I hope not. Between the hours of play I have to be completely objective. Afterwards the friendship resumes, hopefully.

VM: What about the reverse situation? For instance, on my first tour – to Australia – Foxy was very standoffish towards the press, having obeyed the management's pre-tour warning to the letter – so obviously he didn't endear himself to you all. Might the reports of his performance have been coloured by this animosity?

PS: There's some truth in that. Foxy ignored us for six weeks and when things were going against him, he didn't, perhaps get the sympathy that he would otherwise have done.

VM: As you know, Foxy was a victim of his own inexperience of touring. Before we left England we were told in no uncertain terms that it was a waste of time, if not dangerous, to spend hours in the bar with the press and Foxy, who didn't know many of the journalists anyway, was very suspicious. Both Bob Willis and Doug Insole were very wary of you as a body. You finally intervened, didn't you?

PS: Yes. I had a meal with Doug Insole and said that this kid was suffering unnecessarily. Ian Botham had told me that Cathy (Ian's wife) had received a phone call from Foxy's wife, who was distraught at some of the things written about Graeme. I explained that Foxy hadn't spoken a word to us so we may not have been totally sympathetic towards him.

VM: After that, the management called a meeting to tell us, at least be civil to the press so that we could co-exist reasonably together. It was all very confusing for first tourists. Do you think the management of that tour overemphasised the dangers of fraternising with the press?

PS: Of course I do. I think their attitude made it unnecessarily difficult for both sides. As you know, Foxy now has a good relationship with us.

VM: Do you think that the English press are more critical and less enthusiastic than their counterparts in Australia, for example?

PS: We are more critical but not as hard. The Aussie press go beserk if they win – and if they lose. We tend to avoid the extremes. Often contentious topics are created by the TV and radio. At home we frequently get office interference from those watching and listening to the pundits on the TV and radio. Last year at Old Trafford when Paul Terry was injured, England followed on and Foxy was out second ball and there was a considerable delay before Paul Downton came out. In the critical mood that existed at the time, Ray Illingworth on TV suggested that perhaps England hadn't even worked out who should bat at number three. So my office phoned me to tell me to investigate this with the thought in mind of an England in such chaos they haven't even got a batting order worked out story. I already knew that this wasn't true and that Paul had been told of his promotion before arriving at the ground. But because Ray had said it on TV they wouldn't believe me until I'd checked it out again. Often the severest criticisms stem from players like Denis Compton, Ted Dexter and Fred Trueman. I can remember working with Ken Barrington soon after his retirement from the *Daily Sketch*. We had had a lousy day's play at Lord's with England scoring 210 runs off about 100 overs. Ken said 'I can't stand watching this rubbish!' I reminded him that we had to watch him doing exactly the same thing for twenty years. To his credit he replied, 'You're absolutely right, Peter'.

VM: Back to the present – could you give me your impressions of this touring party?

PS: It's a tremendous effort to come back from one down in India. Even in September I wrote that a young side would benefit England on a tour here – not having three or four old stayers who didn't like India and who would have probably affected the attitude of the youngsters.

I've found the whole spirit of the side refreshing. For the first time in all the tours I've covered I don't think I've found a touring side that's been so united. Usually there are two or three moaners but you haven't one. Henri was always a potential problem, but even though he's naturally a loner he's mucked in whenever he's had to.

VM: As a group, because we're all very much on a par in terms of age and experience, people have been more confident and prepared to be their own man than on many previous tours.

PS: Yes that's a veiled reference to Ian Botham and Bob Willis. Willis was occasionally very remote and Ian will rule a dressing room. He'll impose his influence and unwittingly he can inhibit everyone so that they don't always say what they feel. Haven't you all felt that you can express whatever you think?

VM: Yes the likes of Elly and Robbo have felt no need to conform to any pre-ordained norm (and have been more confident as a result).

At this point I realised that we had begun to revert to our normal roles with Peter asking the questions so I stopped my tape recorder and left, promising to buy this affable old pro a drink if we happened to meet at the bar between now and March.

So far on this tour there has been an easy relationship between the press and the players, which will always be the case if we play well. Yet even after the first month, when we were mediocre I noticed that John Thicknesse in the *Cricketer* wrote, 'And, praise be, the Willis era over, players were revisiting the Press tent to pass the time of day'. So all is peace and harmony – until the next playing calamity occurs.

I had better mention the match against South Zone, though I do not recall it with any relish. Others may, especially Martyn Moxon. In only his third innings of the tour he compiled an excellent 153, a performance which would have probably earned him a Test spot on most tours, though I doubt that it will here. Jon Agnew, in his first match, was our most wayward and our most penetrating bowler, taking 7–205 in the match off 45 overs. In between a few rusty half-volleys his willowy frame hurtled down some quick ones and by the end of the match both he and Martyn were grateful that our hotel was one of the better ones, which boasted a bath and hot water. Neither have been accustomed to such vigorous exercise recently.

However I didn't have to exert myself a great deal, which annoyed me. Most people on most tours have a low period when the cricket goes wrong and no-one seems to understand. This happened to me at Hyderabad. Inevitably some of the wounds were self-inflicted: in our first innings I hit my second ball from South Zone's left-arm spinner into first slip's right hand. But my main concern was that I bowled only eight overs throughout the four days, which would comprise my only cricket between 21 December and 20 January. How was I expected to be anywhere near my peak for the one-day games after the Madras Test with such limited practice? They must have more confidence in my ability to find some sort of bowling of them at will than I have. Notice that I've already ruled myself out of the Madras Test and that I'm beginning to regard myself as the one-day specialist. As the tour has progressed both Pat Pocock and I have – reluctantly – been categorised as 5-day/1-day specialists. Yet Pat has an excellent one-day record for Surrey and I nearly did the double last year. I admit that my one-day record may have been the decisive factor in my selection for the last three overseas tours, but the prospect of being shunted around the globe for four and a half months every winter just to play in half a dozen one-day games, does not always fill me with great excitement. I know the answer is to take a hatful of wickets in the longer games but at Hyderabad I didn't feel that I was given the chance.

So for much of the game I plodded from mid-on to third man wondering why my services were being ignored. Maybe if I was a more forceful character, who exuded confidence, I'd have bowled more overs. But the 'give me the ball, I'll bowl this lot out' approach has not been characteristic of Marks on a cricket field over the years; I'm all too aware of the possibility of failing to run through the opposition and looking a twit. Several of those close to me have complained of my lack of self-belief and they're probably right. On the fourth day I mentioned to Norman Gifford that I considered our tactics to be shortsighted, but otherwise I withdrew into my shell, never a very fruitful reaction, but a characteristic one. I suppose I was mildly cheered when I managed to avoid a pair in the last afternoon.

SOUTH ZONE v ENGLAND XI

Played at Gymkhana Ground, Secunderabad. January 7, 8, 9, 10
Toss: ENGLAND XI Match Drawn

SOUTH ZONE

*K. Srikkanth	c Moxon b Agnew	90	(3) lbw b Cowdrey	18
M. Srinivasaprasad	c French b Agnew	0	(1) lbw b Foster	18
†S. Viswanath	c Gatting b Foster	34	(2) c sub (G. Fowler) b Agnew	12
R. Madhavan	c Edmonds b Foster	0	c French b Cowdrey	13
M. Azharuddin	b Agnew	18	(7) c French b Edmonds	52
R. M. H. Binny	b Agnew	19	b Cowdrey	14
R. Kanwilkar	c French b Cowdrey	21	(8) c Cowdrey b Agnew	9
K. A. Qayyum	c Edmonds b Cowans	18	(5) b Foster	39
Arshad Ayub	c French b Foster	58	not out	35
W. V. Raman	lbw b Agnew	26	not out	24
T. A. Sekar	not out	0		
Extras	(LB10 NB12)	22	(B4 LB2 NB19)	25
Total		306	(8 wkts dec)	259

Fall of Wickets:
1st Innings: 1–7, 2–62, 3–62, 4–131, 5–157, 6–174, 7–200, 8–234, 9–306, 10–306.
2nd Innings: 1–29, 2–48, 3–52, 4–67, 5–100, 6–143, 7–168, 8–210.

Bowling:
1st Innings: Cowans 9–2–37–1; Agnew 19–1–102–5; Foster 19.4–6–45–3; Edmonds 13–7–28–0; Marks 7–2–27–0; Cowdrey 11–1–44–1; Gatting 3–0–13–0.
2nd Innings: Agnew 26–3–103–2; Foster 24–8–49–2; Cowdrey 22–5–61–3; Gatting 3–0–3–0; Edmonds 10–3–32–1; Marks 1–0–5–0.

ENGLAND XI

M. D. Moxon	b Raman	153	c Viswanath b Kanwilkar	0
R. T. Robinson	c Raman b Sekar	13	run out	32
*D. I. Gower	c Srinivasaprasad b Sekar	13	c Kanwilkar b Raman	41
C. S. Cowdrey	c Srikkanth b Arshad Ayub	22	b Raman	6
M. W. Gatting	c Kanwilkar b Raman	50	not out	30
V. J. Marks	c Srinivasaprasad b Raman	0	(7) not out	11
†B. N. French	c Kanwilkar b Arshad Ayub	1	(6) c Viswanath b Arshad Ayub	11
P. H. Edmonds	c Srinivasaprasad b Raman	29		
N. A. Foster	c Viswanath b Sekar	29		
J. P. Agnew	not out	12		
N. G. Cowans	c Azharuddin b Raman	0		
Extras	(LB5 NB7)	12	(NB1)	1
Total		334	(5 wkts)	132

Fall of Wickets:
1st Innings: 1–18, 2–45, 3–88, 4–176, 5–176, 6–179, 7–226, 8–297, 9–332, 10–334.
2nd Innings: 1–1, 2–72, 3–80, 4–80, 5–102.

Bowling:
1st Innings: Sekar 24–4–74–3; Binny 11–1–41–0; Kanwilkar 12–3–28–0; Arshad Ayub 34–4–116–2; Raman 28.4–11–59–5; Srinivasaprasad 1–0–8–0; Srikkanth 1–0–3–0.
2nd Innings: Sekar 7–2–17–0; Kanwilkar 4–0–20–1; Arshad Ayub 10–0–48–1; Raman 8–0–39–2; Srikkanth 1–0–8–0.

Umpires: S. K. Ghosh and S. R. Ramachandra Rao.

11
Madras

Test matches rarely follow the course outlined by the captain at team meetings – unless the captain happens to be Clive Lloyd, but the Fourth Test at Madras proved to be an exception. On the eve of the game, David Gower suggested that this would be the decisive Test of the series: the venue for the final Test at Kanpur was renowned for producing dull, lifeless draws, whereas the wicket at Madras usually provided initial bounce for the seamers and some turn for the spinners in the later stages. We felt that India had finally selected their strongest possible side; Kapil was back and Gaekwad had been replaced by the more unpredictable and certainly more dangerous Srikkanth, yet there remained chinks of vulnerability; our main batsmen were now confident of thwarting Siva, India's prime attacking force and their astonishing batting collapse in Delhi had yet to be fully exorcised. At some stage we had to bat for two days and recreate the atmosphere of Delhi. England made one change: Richard Ellison had never properly recovered from his marathon spell at Calcutta and was replaced by Neil Foster. Neil had bowled effectively at Hyderabad and we all felt that he would do a reliable job, but none of us, except perhaps Neil himself, thought that he would be the most influential player on the field.

Madras is to Calcutta what Bournemouth is to Birmingham. There are beggars and slums but they are far less obtrusive and less in number than in the northern cities. The city is blessed with a long beach front along the Bay of Bengal, the streets are broad and according to my guidebook, it is possible to use public buses without undue discomfort. Your intrepid reporter decided not to test the accuracy of this assertion, but I was certainly impressed by the efficiency of the Tamil Nadu cricket authorities. There were excellent net facilities plus a gaggle of quality bowlers, most of whom were budding Sivaramakrishnans, despite being twice his age. Siva is from Madras and several locals expressed surprise at his success; in district cricket he is merrily walloped to the mid-wicket boundary but he scores a stack of runs. This does not altogether surprise me. I used to play village cricket in Somerset and my cunning off-breaks were treated with disdain and I am certain that if I returned to the village green now, after all my lofty experiences, the same thing would happen, unless some clever dick recognised the MCC touring sweater.

Often spinners rely upon the enormity of the occasion and the ragged nerve ends of the batsmen for their success. In three Lord's finals my bowling has been treated with remarkable suspicion and a few gentle half-volleys have been patted to mid-off with acute relief. The true village cricketer has no such inhibitions. If he can see it, he whacks it – as far as possible.

The stadium is an impressive, functional oval bowl marred only by the proximity of the city sewers and there, on 13 January, Gavaskar won the toss and elected to bat.

As he strode out to the wicket with Srikkanth I went up into the stands and sat next to Syed Kirmani, who was eager to have a close look at England's fresh opening bowler. India's little wicketkeeper, a veteran now of eighty Test matches, is a gentle implacable character full of Eastern calm and charm, yet even he was on the edge of his seat for an hour as we were immediately transported back to the atmosphere of the second day at Bombay. Foster's first ball in Test cricket for six months was just short of a length outside off stump. Gavaskar jumped onto the back foot and drove him through the vacant mid-off area for four. Foster bounced him and for the first time in the series Gavaskar hooked – with complete authority. Ten runs came from the over and I asked Kirmani what was going on; after all, this was a Test match. He replied that Gavaskar had sought advice on how he should combat his unusual run of failures in this series. 'Play your shots', had been Kirmani's response – it was now Gavaskar's.

The pressure on Foster was a little different. He abhors long periods of inactivity on tour more than most and this was his first chance to re-establish himself as England's opening bowler. Neil has innate confidence in his ability to bowl and a refreshingly straightforward opinion of his worth. Without a trace of arrogance he told me, 'I thought I should play in this Test match, even though I wasn't sure that I would.' He does not usually suffer from nerves, but he admitted to being a 'little apprehensive' after that first over. 'I'd seen how they sometimes attack the new ball in this series and I had no cover at all, no mid-off or third man.' Gavaskar scored India's first 17 runs and appeared to be bristling with confidence, no doubt mindful of his brilliant double century here against the West Indians the year before. However, in his third over, Foster bowled a straight full length ball, Gavaskar aimed to clip it through mid wicket, missed it and was bowled. 'Did it swing Neil?' 'Probably not – just an awful shot.' I told you about the Essex seamer's straightforward honesty.

Soon after his dismissal, Sunil emerged from the dressing room and sat himself down next to Norman Gifford, in a slightly perplexed frame of mind. A few years ago, he would have brooded in the dressing room for hours, analysing his errors and agonising over his failure, but not any more, and this change worried him. He refused to admit to staleness as he had spent five months away from cricket during the English summer, yet the thrill of success, and more importantly, the desperation of failure now eluded him and that was a bad sign. He was the father figure, the confidant of the young players in the Indian side and was happy to pass on to Azharuddin and Siva the fruits of his experience, but who was *his* confidant? At Bombay, the Indian team manager was Raj Singh who could fulfil that role but at every centre the manager had changed and now there was a void. It occurred to me that not many players of his stature would admit to such weaknesses and I admired him for it.

Meanwhile, the game progressed at breakneck pace. Srikkanth, unsure whether to block or blast on his recall, was caught behind for a duck and Vengsarkar, still tentative, edged Foster to Lamb at second slip and India were 45–3. The pattern of the previous Tests now established itself as Amarnath and Azharuddin blunted the English new ball threat with immense confidence. Cowans bowled a bouncer and Amarnath hooked it imperiously for six. Whilst Cowans has achieved a certain mastery over Vengsarkar in this series, Amarnath has dominated Cowans. Mohinder has a remarkable Test record against pace: in the West Indies, he was described as the best player of fast bowling in the world – by the West Indians – and yet in India last year in six Test innings against Marshall and Co. he produced one run and five ducks and his inevitable omission. Now he is back to peak form and after lunch he showed his relish for the spinners as he took eighteen from an over from Phil Edmonds so that Gower was forced to turn to the medium pace of Chris Cowdrey. Remarkably, on that steamy afternoon, Cowdrey, no more than an occasional change bowler for Kent, found himself holding the England attack together along with Neil Foster. The spinners had been rendered ineffective by Mohinder's assault and Cowans' bowling is not suited to long containing spells. The two batsmen sensed their opportunity; the wicket encouraged stroke play with its generous even bounce, the outfield was fast and the heat oppressive and yet, within the space of twenty minutes, the match had lurched in England's favour. To everyone's surprise Cowdrey bowled Azharuddin whereupon Foster and Downton combined to dismiss Amarnath ('it bounced and swung') and Shastri ('caught behind swishing wasn't he' said Foster in his unmistakable Essex burr).

This heightened the drama as the new batsman was Kapil Dev on his recall. How would he react to the crisis? Would we see a now chastened Kapil? His first over from Cowdrey provided the answer. To his first ball he played a lofted extra cover drive which just skimmed over the outstretched arms of Tim Robinson; he slashed at his third and the ball flew between Lamb and Gatting in the slips; he then played and missed twice before lofting the final delivery over mid-on for four. The message was simple – 'I'm not changing for anyone'. Kapil continued in this vein scoring 50 from 60 balls in 73 minutes, whereupon he was superbly caught at long-off by Cowans off the drenched persevering Cowdrey – an unusual mode of dismissal on the first day of a Test match.

Foster, now partnered by Cowans, ensured that there would be no last ditch resistance and India were bowled out for 272 in just 68 overs, an astonishing 4½ hours of Test cricket. Neil's figures were 23–2–104–6. However did he manage that considering that his previous twelve Test wickets had cost more than 50 each? 'I always felt I could get them out as the ball bounced and swung a little. It was my wicket. Of all the bowlers in the match and there were better than me on show – like Kapil – I was the most dangerous because of my height and high action. I could get the ball to bounce more than the others. But I was amazed how impetuous they were.' So was everyone else; it had provided superb entertainment but it was no way to win a vital Test match. After just four hours we sensed a golden opportunity to snatch a Test match victory, thanks to the bowling of Foster and Cowdrey. Chris's nineteen consecutive overs had revealed hitherto unknown reserves of stamina but they did provide one problem. He had created a large area of rough just outside the left-hander's off stump, ideal for Siva's leg breaks. Two years ago this may have posed insurmountable problems for Graeme Fowler.

I have been able to observe Graeme's Test career at close quarters. We both made our debut in August 1982 against Pakistan at Headingley, where Graeme's plucky 86 in the second innings ensured a trip to Australia. That tour exposed considerable limitations in both of us as cricketers; just now, indeed at any time, I'd prefer to concentrate on Graeme's. He has a sharp analytical mind and has learnt from that experience. Let him explain: 'I'd only played two seasons for Lancashire when I went to Australia and I'd received very little coaching except from David Lloyd but suddenly after one game for England, simply everyone wanted to coach me, especially since I'd been labelled in the press as an unorthodox player. So in Australia I tried to play as I thought an England player should and I didn't score a run. Everyone tried to help but I don't think that I was mature enough to succeed on that tour. It was only after talking to Clive Lloyd that I began to see the light. He said that batting should be an extension of your personality and that I should not desert the method that had made me an England player; gradually technical deficiencies would be ironed out but to attempt a complete overhaul was madness. So then I went back to playing like I did for Lancashire.'

I should point out that Graeme's tour was not a complete cricketing disaster. At Brisbane, 'batting like an England player', he scored 80 against Thomson and Rackemann, an innings memorable for its courage and determination rather than its fluency. At Melbourne, and adopting his Lancashire style, he scored 60, smiting Yardley for three lofted boundaries in one over in response to a collective decision before the match to attack the off-spinner. Late in that innings his foot was broken and to all intents and purposes that was the end of his tour.

In New Zealand the following year he was still unable to establish himself as England's regular opener, despite scoring 100 and an 80 at Palmerston North. The selectors preferred the more dogged virtues of Tavare and Chris Smith. Graeme's technique, though effective, did not inspire confidence. I nicknamed one of his shots 'the flail', a sort of front foot explosion that could deposit the ball anywhere between cover point and square leg. It was too easy to focus on this aspect of his play rather than his improving defensive technique. However, his resilient display against the West Indies in the summer of 1984 including a century at Lord's earned him a winter trip as England's senior opener since neither of his prospective partners had ever played in a Test match. Yet in September he had lukewarm feelings towards touring: 'The first tour was like a novelty, on the second I was conversant with my surroundings and what was required, but I wasn't really looking forward to the third: I wanted to spend some time at home.' I suspect that most regular tourists feel the same, but the logical response – declining the invitation – has rarely been pursued since the abolition of the amateur.

Yet, he has been far more successful on this tour, culminating in his magnificent innings at Madras. He attributes this to playing regularly in the early part of the tour and being an automatic selection for the First Test. He enjoys the added responsibility of being a senior member of the side. 'I like the fact that I am not the kid of the touring party as I was in Australia because if people look to me to score runs or field well as at Lancashire, then I'm far more likely to do so. When I'm "young Fowler" there's too much leeway to fail.' By the time we reached Madras his team-mates certainly expected runs from him.

For the first hour of his innings he was very aware of the rough and worried by the prospect of unpredictable bounce. However, Siva, on his home ground, was also very conscious of the patch and as a result put greater pressure on himself. Fowler sensed this: 'Siva was disappointed after every over if he hadn't beaten the bat and exploited the rough. Where I was impetuous twelve or eighteen months ago, he was impetuous in Madras.' Gradually the threat of the rough receded – maybe our left-handers had been oversensitive about it as they glowered at the offending patch for several minutes on the second morning, and as the opening partnership began to flourish Graeme decided to ignore it. Fowler's patience outlasted that of the little Indian leg spinner. In Calcutta he had been dismissed trying to flick a full-length ball through mid-wicket so at Madras he decided to deadbat full-length deliveries, maybe picking up singles to square leg, and await short balls: steadily these became more frequent so that the Indians had to fall back on the more orthodox wiles of their other bowlers.

'We must bat for two days', had been the cry at the team meeting. The Indians had used excellent batting conditions wantonly and it was imperative that we should not make the same mistake. We didn't. Our first four batsmen alone batted for two days. Just reflect on the scoreboard at various stages of the English innings for you will not see their like again, 178–0, 419–1, 563–2.

On the second day, Tim Robinson, methodical and imperturbable, was the only batsman to be dismissed, nicking a perfect legspinner to the wicketkeeper and on the third day the demolition exercise of the Indian attack continued ruthlessly. Fowler and Gatting took no obvious risks until after lunch when Graeme lofted Yadav for two sixes in an over, the second of which took him to 198. I think one is probably entitled to use the aerial route when on 186, even in a Test match. However, soon after Graeme had reached his double century England plummeted to 419–2 when he was caught behind off Kapil. He was disappointed as he had wanted to beat his old friend and mentor David Lloyd's career best score of 214. Once Foxy had reached a hundred, he realised what a golden opportunity there was for a really big score. England needed to bat for a long time, the wicket was true and the bowlers gradually resigned to simply containing the batsmen rather than dismissing them – so why stop at 201? Still it is a superb achievement to bat for nine and a half hours whatever the conditions and it is interesting to note his observations of his two batting partners, 'Robbo gains his concentration from silence; he doesn't like to chat in between overs. He might come down the wicket to mention what a particular bowler is doing or to note a field change, but otherwise he'll stay at his end and gather his thoughts. He's a little like Chris Tavare at the wicket, obviously steeling himself to concentrate. Mike Gatting, in contrast, is so enthusiastic, so full of hyped-up aggression; he talks and encourages constantly between overs. This steady barrage may annoy Robbo, but I often find it helpful, especially if I'm tired.' At the end of the second day, Graeme was very tired and during the final half-hour was obviously clinging on to his wicket, unconcerned about scoring runs. In the final over an obvious single was rejected so that Gatting should take responsibility for the last four balls of the day. It was an unselfish gesture by England's vice-captain, for self-centred cricketers always avoid the last over of the day if possible – there's nothing to gain.

After Graeme's dismissal, Allan Lamb carefully established himself at the crease and one Indian in the stand was heard muttering, 'Oh my God! The worst disaster since Bhopal'. By now Gatting could have been playing against Somerset at Bath facing Marks. Several times he reverse lapped Shastri, tearing up Ian Botham's English copyright on the shot, which is cricket's equivalent of riding a Derby winner home sidesaddle. Finally, having completed a chanceless double-century, his masterful innings ended as he attempted to hit

Shastri for another straight six. His dismissal introduced a new concept to Test cricket, the offensive night-watchman, a role played with much relish by Phil Edmonds.

So, by the next day, three of our number, Foster, Fowler and Gatting, had performed heroics on the cricket field. Yet none of their deeds can possibly equal those of Jon Agnew and Bruce French. Given the day off, they opted to go to Fisherman's Cove, a beach resort, there being no mountains readily available for Bruce. As they waded into the sea, they heard cries for 'help' from a group of local college girls, two of whom were being dragged out by the strong current. Our two noble heroes immediately swam to the rescue and eventually managed to bring the dazed victims back to the shore. By the evening, Jon, a master of understatement, explained whilst quietly sipping his beer that, 'it was nothing really – I can't understand why the *Daily Mirror* should cover its front page with the story'. Two Indian damsels will hold a different view for the rest of their lives.

On the fourth morning, England added 41 in 5 overs, whereupon Gower declared at 652–7 with a lead of 380. So far, everything had gone according to plan, yet the question remained: 'Could England and Neil Foster bowl them out again on a surface that showed no signs of deteriorating?' 'No, I didn't think I could', was Neil's reply, 'I'd never got ten wickets in a match in a county game, let alone a Test match'. Within three-quarters of an hour he had mustered nine as India were reduced to 22–3. Gavaskar edged a perfect bouncing away swinger to first slip, Vengsarkar was fortuitously caught down the leg side and Srikkanth . . .

'Srikkanth had just hooked Flash (Cowans) for a top-edged six – having hardly bowled a ball to him in the innings, I then had him at my end for two overs on the trot', Neil told me afterwards. 'I just pitched it up to him because the ball was swinging again and I thought my best chance was a catch behind the wicket. So having got him coming forward, I thought "let's try it". I didn't attempt an authentic bouncer, but I shut my eyes, grunted and banged it in as quick as I could and he did the right thing.' The right thing was spooning the ball tamely to Cowdrey at backward short leg as he was hurried into an attempted hook shot, which all goes to show that you don't have to bowl at less than 50 mph to have guile. Ask Fred Trueman.

Now Amarnath and Azharuddin staged the usual middle order recovery, not by dogged defence but by trusting their natural aggressive instincts; even the most obdurate of blockers could not fail to hit boundaries on this surface and this outfield. Only Foster was treated with suspicion and respect. When Pocock was introduced Amarnath swung him over mid on and Azharuddin repeatedly made room to cut. For the first time in four days England were losing their grip on the match. Azharuddin was more fluent than at Calcutta, loitering on the back foot before deciding whether to drive through extra cover or, if he preferred, mid wicket. He continued to torment Pocock, who later declared that he'd never been so depressed about his bowling in 20 years of first-class cricket. But Percy being Percy, this depression was short-lived. Just when we were resigning ourselves to Amarnath's first century of the series and a sizeable problem on the last day, Foster induced Amarnath to mishook (at last) and Cowans, staring into the sun, clung on to the ball at long leg. For someone who is awful at catching practice, Norman has a remarkably safe pair of hands. At least I'm consistent.

So six wickets were needed on the final day. Gower shrewdly delayed taking the second new ball and opened with his spinners. Pocock rediscovered his rhythm, whilst Henri was persuaded to experiment by bowling over the wicket. He had been encouraged to try this ploy by Norman Gifford, who is a master at lobbing the ball outside the right-hander's leg stump into the rough. In English county cricket, Norman enjoys teasing the best batsmen with this tactic; either they can sweep to the well-policed leg-side field, gambling upon even bounce or they have to adopt the unnatural and undignified policy of kicking the ball away.

Henri finds it difficult to toss the ball up slowly but he tried it a little reluctantly on the fifth morning. Initially the ploy worked. After Azharuddin, having scored his second Test century, had been snapped up at silly point by Gower, Henri made one ball rear viciously from the rough to smack Shastri's gloves. However, when Kapil and Kirmani responded with a series of lofted drives Henri became frustrated bowling over the wicket and reverted to his orthodox method. Finally, as the Indian counter-attack flourished he tried his chinaman, which Kapil disdainfully cut for four whereupon Norman Gifford declared, 'Not even at my flamboyant best would I have tried that'. Henri's chinamen have not been altogether successful on this tour; rarely have they escaped being hit for four, but some day he will take a Test wicket with a wrist spinner and the sacrifice will be deemed worthwhile. The old amateur spirit lingers on in Edmonds and as the tour progressed and the bones began to ache, he expressed the view that he would like to play for England next year and for Finchley CC at the weekends; that would be his ideal life-style, though Mike Gatting was not totally enamoured with the idea.

Gower now summoned the new ball, with Cowans and Foster, and Flash soon ended Kapil's typically flamboyant innings by having him caught at slip and just before lunch Foster, trapping Siva lbw, captured his eleventh wicket in the match. After a noisy, animated interval, Cowans dismissed Yadav and an innings victory seemed imminent. However, Chetan Sharma and Kirmani frustrated us for 85 minutes: the pace bowlers delivered a succession of bouncers, but Kirmani kept leaning back and slashing them over gully. Finally, Edmonds was recalled and bowling around the wicket he induced Kirmani to sky an attempted drive to Allan Lamb at cover point for a defiant 75. On his return to the pavilion Henri, tongue in cheek, announced to Gifford, 'I told you I was better off bowling around the wicket'. We needed just 33 to win. Siva, opening the bowling, finally got the better of Fowler, but Robinson and Gatting guided us serenely to victory.

In the dressing room there was naturally jubilation and a release of tension after five days of stern self-discipline. It had been a perfect, thoroughly professional performance with everyone contributing something, but now the team could be frivolous and carefree for a while. Our victory had coincided with the tea interval; a few cream cakes were devoured but the majority flew across the room and for some reason were attracted like a magnet to Jon Agnew's head. Photographers, officials and wives appeared along with some champagne, which swiftly disappeared down people's gullets, over people's hair and into my cricket case. Foster, Fowler and Gatting were summoned by the English press photographers, who had no difficulty extracting pictures of joy and exultation.

Those of us not playing in the game were more restrained. Of course we were thrilled by the victory and proud of the side but no matter how much importance is attached to the contribution of the 'backroom boys', it is impossible to relish victory to the same extent as those actively involved. Apart from Jon, we dodged the cream missiles successfully and quietly sipped champagne, but we could not quite muster the same euphoria. I don't think we were being disloyal, just human.

Back at the Taj Coromandel, the hotel manager produced some more champagne for room 705, where we were joined by members of the English press. He was an excellent host. At the end of day two, Graeme Fowler having scored a century found his room adorned with bouquets of flowers and a massive chocolate cake. After day three, these gifts were augmented by more flowers and champagne for Foxy and Mike Gatting. The hotel manager was obviously a cricket enthusiast and, I daresay, a batsman, as Neil Foster's eleven wickets didn't merit a can of beer. That's not meant to sound carping, for anyone who can procure champagne in India is worthy of cultivating the highest admiration.

For Gatting, the match had been the culmination of a triumphant Indian summer; by now his England place had been firmly established. Foster's and Fowler's position had appeared more fragile before the Madras Test. Suddenly there is a glut of potential English opening batsmen: Tim Robinson and, with limited opportunities, Martyn Moxon have impressed greatly on this tour and Graham Gooch is available next summer. Unusually the competition will be fierce and a double century will have helped to adjust the usual assessment of Graeme's batting – 'lucky, unorthodox with technical deficiencies that are countered by his resolute temperament'. Indeed the Madras Test threw up one remarkable statistic. After twenty Tests, Graeme has scored more runs than most of England's leading batsmen over the same period, 100 more than Boycott and Edrich, 150 more than Graveney and Randall, 200 more than Gooch, 300 more than Fletcher. He can't be that bad a player.

Neil Foster has yet to play more than two consecutive Tests for England and though he has bowled impressively overseas, he has been ineffective at home. For Essex, he is sometimes required to perform a different role than for England. Whilst the indefatigable John Lever, along with Derek Pringle and perhaps Stuart Turner, bowl a full length, Neil often acts as the intimidator, who has to shake up the more timorous souls in county cricket, by bowling as fast as he can. This may benefit the side but can produce harmful side effects for Neil; a loss of control and a tendency to bowl too short. His ambition now is to play three Tests consecutively against Australia next summer so that he can have a prolonged opportunity to prove his worth. After his performance at Madras, few would begrudge him this chance, but cricket, as they say, is a 'funny' game; success is often illusory and goals are often shattered. Ask Paul Allott.

INDIA v ENGLAND (FOURTH TEST MATCH)

Played at M. A. Chidambaram Stadium, Chepauk, Madras
January 13, 14, 15, 17, 18
Toss: INDIA ENGLAND won by 9 wickets

INDIA

*S. M. Gavaskar	b Foster	17	c Gatting b Foster	3
K. Srikkanth	c Downton b Cowans	0	c Cowdrey b Foster	16
D. B. Vengsarkar	c Lamb b Foster	17	c Downton b Foster	2
M. Amarnath	c Downton b Foster	78	c Cowans b Foster	95
M. Azharuddin	b Cowdrey	48	c Gower b Pocock	105
R. J. Shastri	c Downton b Foster	2	c Cowdrey b Edmonds	33
Kapil Dev	c Cowans b Cowdrey	53	c Gatting b Cowans	49
†S. M. H. Kirmani	not out	30	c Lamb b Edmonds	75
N. S. Yadav	b Foster	2	(10) c Downton b Cowans	5
L. Sivaramakrishnan	c Cowdrey b Foster	13	(9) lbw b Foster	5
C. Sharma	c Lamb b Cowans	5	not out	17
Extras	(LB3 NB4)	7	(B1 LB4 NB2)	7
Total		272		412

Fall of Wickets:
1st Innings: 1–17, 2–17, 3–45, 4–155, 5–167, 6–167, 7–241, 8–243, 9–263, 10–272.
2nd Innings: 1–7, 2–19, 3–22, 4–212, 5–259, 6–259, 7–341, 8–350, 9–361, 10–412.

Bowling:
1st Innings: Cowans 12.5–3–39–2; Foster 23–2–104–6; Edmonds 6–1–33–0; Cowdrey 19–1–65–2; Pocock 7–1–28–0.
2nd Innings: Cowans 15–1–73–2; Foster 28–8–59–5; Cowdrey 5–0–26–0; Edmonds 41.5–13–119–2; Pocock 33–8–130–1.

ENGLAND

G. Fowler	c Kirmani b Kapil Dev	201	c Kirmani b Sivaramakrishnan	2
R. T. Robinson	c Kirmani b Sivaramakrishnan	74	not out	21
M. W. Gatting	c sub (G. Sharma) b Shastri	207	not out	10
A. J. Lamb	b Amarnath	62		
P. H. Edmonds	lbw b Shastri	36		
N. A. Foster	b Amarnath	5		
*D. I. Gower	b Kapil Dev	18		
C. S. Cowdrey	not out	3		
†P. R. Downton	not out	3		
P. I. Pocock N. G. Cowans	did not bat			
Extras	(B7 LB19 NB17)	43	(LB1 W1)	2
Total	(7 wkts dec)	652	(1 wkt)	35

Fall of Wickets:
1st Innings: 1–178, 2–419, 3–563, 4–599, 5–604, 6–640, 7–646.
2nd Innings: 1–7.

Bowling:
1st Innings: Kapil Dev 36–5–131–2; Sharma 18–0–95–0; Sivaramakrishnan 44–6–145–1; Yadav 23–4–76–0; Shastri 42–7–143–2; Amarnath 12–1–36–2.
2nd Innings: Kapil Dev 3–0–20–0; Sivaramakrishnan 4–0–12–1; Shastri 1–0–2–0.

Umpires: M. Y. Gupte and V. K. Ramaswamy.

12

Bangalore – Nagpur – Chandigarh

No doubt you have imagined us relaxing by the pool in blazing sunshine on the day after the Fourth Test match, merrily reliving some of its memorable moments. Not a bit of it. Our new itinerary is remarkably condensed; it has virtually the same number of fixtures as the original but in two weeks less. So at 5.15 a.m. I bade a reluctant farewell to my wife and boarded the coach to the airport before flying to Bangalore, where we breakfasted at 7.30 a.m. By 10 a.m. we were in the nets in preparation for the third one-day international.

In the afternoon I retired to my room intending to catch up with this diary but I fell asleep with the pen in my hand and, to my chagrin, was late for our team meeting at 6 p.m. I should mention my writing as it has usurped many hours of my spare time on this tour. On occasions I've found it a welcome escape and a fresh challenge especially when I've been omitted from Test sides; the book's completion – to my noble publisher's satisfaction – has provided an alternative goal. At other times it has been burdensome and has restricted my freedom. I've discovered that any tourist with literary pretensions needs considerable self-discipline and it helps to be teetotal or at least anti-social: the attractions of the team room or the hotel bar have to be shunned on occasions – I'm not sure I'm ideally suited to this role. Alternatively you need an excellent ghost-writer. I used to despise all ghost-written cricket books but not any more. Anyway please read on, if only to discover whether we reach Heathrow together.

At the team meeting, there were the usual observations. 'Don't bowl at Sharen's or Gavaskar's legs; mid-off should be ten yards deeper for Srikkanth, bowl a full length at off stump to Azharuddin, we must have wickets in hand, keep your eye on the captain and let's take the pressure off ourselves by winning the one-day series at the first attempt.' However, there was one unusual feature. At the beginning of the meeting there was no team announcement. Just before we broke up, Pat Pocock asked: 'By the way, who's playing?' It had simply been taken for granted that the same XII as Cuttack, were selected. This omission reflects the surge in confidence that has overtaken this tour party over the last seven weeks. The selection process had become simple: we just reverted to the one-day formula. None of us had previously experienced such a long run of success for England overseas. After the meeting to round off one of our more exhausting non-playing days on tour we attended a cocktail party given by the local cricket association. The parties on this tour have not been at all onerous. We attend for an hour and a half dressed in tour uniform and the local patriots are always invited. They ask us whether we are enjoying the tour, we ask them how long they have been in India and the conversations stem from there. Inevitably there is a Lancastrian present, who immediately latches onto Graeme Fowler and there begins a survey of the public houses of Blackburn, Wigan and Accrington. Is the North West of England so intolerable that they have all emigrated to India? In Bangalore, Chris Cowdrey was overcome by Indians, claiming to hail from his father's birthplace: most of them appear to have played with or against Colin and they also ask after Tom and Ted. Chris meanwhile retains the smile of a true diplomat. Henri usually ends up with the most influential man in the room whilst Pat Pocock, inheriting 'Chat' Taylor's role, will talk at great length to anybody about anything.

The third day international follows the same pattern as the previous two encounters. The stadium was packed, Gower elected to field and Gavaskar surprisingly chose to split up the successful Srikkanth-Shastri pairing of Cuttack and to open with himself. I suspect that Sunil was anxious to stake a claim for his inclusion for the one-day tournament in Australia, as his hold on the captaincy becomes increasingly fragile. The Indians reached 70–0 and Srikkanth had already cleared my long-on again, whereupon Cowans, to my relief, bowled him. Remember how grumpy I was back at Hyderabad about my lack of bowling and the prospect of being underprepared for the one-day international? Well, it didn't seem to matter. In my second over Gavaskar swept, got a top edge and was caught by Gatting and thereafter I bowled with more control and confidence than at any stage on the tour. Kapil Dev, on his return to the side, mistimed a drive and Gower running behind the umpire caught the skier – for one terrible moment I thought the catch was mine – and Vengsarkar was stumped by yards. Shastri and Azharuddin, who can do no wrong at the moment, improvised cleverly in the final ten overs but 206 from 46 overs seemed a satisfactory target.

However, we made life difficult for ourselves again. There were two unnecessary run-outs, Gower heaved recklessly at Shastri and I did the same to Patil, but Allan Lamb shepherded us (with apologies to literature) towards victory with a clinical assault upon Rajinder Ghai. As a consequence Yashpal Sharma was summoned to bowl his off-spinners off two paces and he delighted us all by bowling three no-balls. As at Poona the crowd reacted to India's imminent defeat by hurling bottles into the outfield and this time Gavaskar led his side off the field, while Lamb and Downton reclined on the square. After twenty minutes and repeated assurances from the ground authorities the Indians returned and we scrambled home with an over to spare. The following day several journalists declared that Gavaskar had over-reacted though I doubt whether they would have reached the same conclusion if one of the bottles had landed upon third man's head.

With hindsight, our victory seems fairly straightforward, yet at the time the match always appeared to be in the balance and the tension showed. If I'm not playing a game I become an avid watcher; during the Test matches I scarcely miss a ball, yet at Bangalore I watched no more than three balls in succession until I was the next man in. For most of us, following the match becomes too draining, too exhausting, so we retreat into the dressing room. Let me briefly try to reconstruct the dressing room scene at Bangalore.

The room itself is spacious with windows looking over the stadium entrance, but not over the playing area: there is a small annexe with a bed and Bernard Thomas our physio is lying there. Bernard, a former Olympic gymnast, is at the ground all the time in case someone goes in the fetlock, but he's not a special connoisseur of cricket and this is now his sixteenth tour. Spread around the room is a mixture of easy and upright chairs plus a sofa and in the middle is a large table where lunch was laid out. Now Lamb, Foster and Edmonds sit there playing cards, an inane game called 'Switch' or 'Last Card', nonetheless they may attract a small audience – anything is better than watching the cricket. They'll keep playing until a wicket falls, not because they are indifferent to the cricket, but because it provides a temporary escape

Bernard Thomas, team physiotherapist, on the shoulders of Norman Cowans.

Bruce French, intrepid explorer.

Pat Pocock, male model

Pat Pocock, male model and 12th man

Phil 'Henri' Edmonds

Neil Foster who took six wickets in the Fourth Test in Madras, January 1985, claims Sunil Gavaskar's wicket. (below)

The scoreboard in the Fourth Test which led ultimately to England clinching the series.

Chris Cowdrey bowls Azharuddin in the Fourth Test

Graeme Fowler edges Sivaramakrishnan through the slips and seven hours later he acknowledges the crowd's applause as he scores a double century.

Meanwhile, Mike Gatting had plenty to smile about and he, too, reached 200.

The author at work and play.

Foxy, Foster and Gatt celebrate after the Fourth Test in Madras

As does the rest of the team

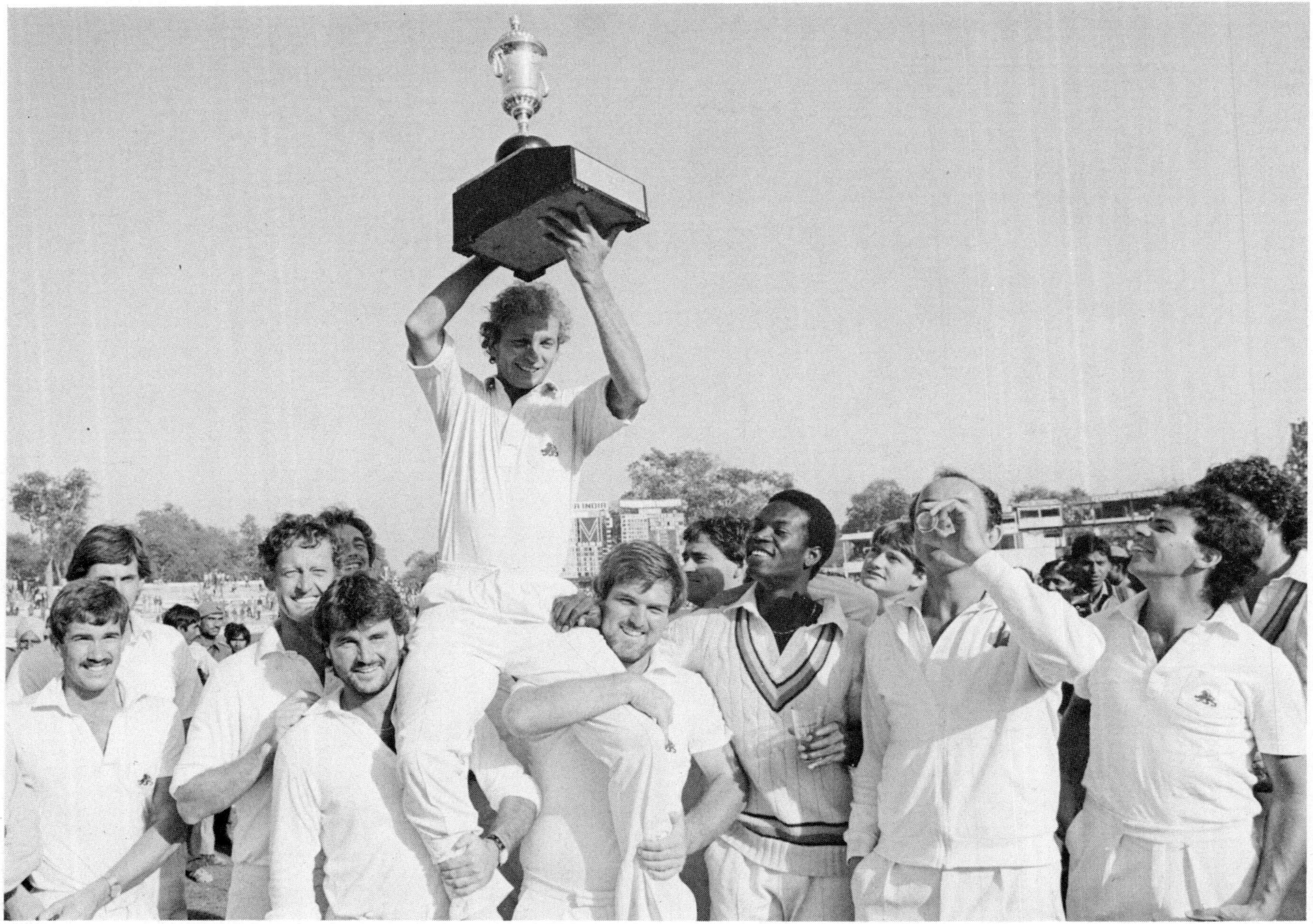

It was worth it all in the end

The team poses

Allan Border, the Australian captain, listens to Bob Hawke, the Australian Prime Minister, talking to David Gower at the opening of the One-Day series in Melbourne, February 1985.

'And the band begins to play . . .'

Cricket, how it could be – Australia v. West Indies under lights at Sydney, February 1985.

Allan Lamb batting during his brilliant innings of 81 against Pakistan – but it was to be in vain.

When am I going to be able to write the next chapter?

from it. Paul Downton sits in an armchair stripped to the waist puffing a panatella. Whilst I hover around the room discovering stray newspapers and staring at them for a few minutes before hovering on. English newspapers are like gold dust – 'After you, after you, don't lose it!' For Richard Ellison a run chase is a rare experience as Kent always bat first: he sits in a corner, consuming countless cigarettes and his stomach aches. Occasionally Henri slips out to the balcony and comes back muttering darkly about 'diabolical' running between the wickets. Topics of conversation range from the latest in house movies to county cricket to snowdrifts in the south of England but we rarely focus on the match in hand until we have to. Every cheer, every groan of the crowd is swiftly interpreted (there's no television here) –'What's that?' 'No, it's OK, it's not loud enough to be a wicket.' If the crowd reaction is indecipherable, someone rushes to the door to seek an explanation. When a roar from the stand signals a wicket, we receive a garbled report from one of the outsiders and the chain moves on. Allan Lamb puts on his pads and disappears to watch, I put on my thigh pads and Paul puts on his whites. The way we play we're bound to get a knock but the sneaking hope remains that we won't.

If only Bernard Shaw, Harold Pinter or Peter Roebuck were here the scene would now burst into dialogue – but they're not. Still, isn't it ridiculous how we torture ourselves? Yet many of us would find cricket, maybe even life so drab and meaningless without this hideous tension. At Bangalore I was glad to be involved again. Spare a thought for the eternal twelfth men, Moxon, French and their new henchman, Agnew.

For the last two and a half weeks an old Oxford friend, the Rev. Andrew Wingfield-Digby, has been following the tour. Andrew opened the bowling for Oxford University in the 1970s at Mohinder Amarnath's pace. Our wicketkeeper, out of deference to the new ball, would stand back for an over before advancing to the stumps. None-theless Andrew became one of Oxford University's most famous characters, if only because of Alan Gibson's kind attentions in the columns of *The Times*, sub-editors viewed him with less affection when he had Ashley Harvey-Walker caught by Kinkead-Weekes off his bowling at Derby. Before the Fourth Test he augmented our net bowlers with his usual unflagging zeal and external optimism, though Andrew, now a regular for Dorset, did confess that the strip at Blandford Forum offered a little more assistance than the Madras net wickets. He has been here to organise a three-week 'Christians in

Sport' tour to South India next October. I hope a few first-class cricketers, including myself, will be participating and any receipts will be donated to the Spastics Society of India. Andrew is now the sole full-time employee of the registered charity 'Christians in Sport' whose aim is to provide a ministry for sportsmen and women. Several football league sides, like Watford, now have a chaplain connected with the club and Andrew would ideally like to broaden the sphere of influence to cricket clubs. His liaison man in India, Pastor Robin Paul, lives in Bangalore and through him we caught a glimpse of India beyond the five-star hotel.

Robin took us to a 'slum' village on the outskirts of Bangalore. As we drove along the track we saw the now familiar sight of women picking through the garbage tips in search of tins, bottles and bottle tops. The village itself did not compare with the scene of horrors that we've seen from a distance in Calcutta and Bombay but to view it at close quarters was an enlightening experience. The open drains attracted swarms of flies and nearby children sat peering curiously at these strange white visitors. There was a constant line of women carrying water jugs upon their heads, returning from one of only four water taps that exist for the population of 5,000 people. We went into one of the shacks, which was 12 ft × 6 ft in size and inside were three children: they were startled at first, but once reassured by our guides they broke into bashful winning smiles, yet I still felt a dreadful intruder. One bed stretched along the width of the dwelling and upon the stone floor shelves held neatly stored containers of food and water and the kerosene lamp. In such cramped conditions order within the home must be essential for a family of five. This was an enterprising household we were told, the father makes and sells bootpolish while the mother sews; meanwhile the children patiently awaited their return. Most of the other inhabitants of the village were casual labourers. Along the path was another familiar Indian sight, that of dung and straw moulded together into the shape of dinner plates and left to dry in the sun. Later these would be used as fuel by the villagers.

This village was established in 1976 on land allotted to those within the boundaries of Bangalore, which is now one of the most attractive and uncluttered Indian cities. Originally all the dwellings were built of wood and thatch but in 1981 there was a fire, which destroyed half of the site, after which the government gave aid to the tune of 2,000 rupees (£1 = 14.5 rupees) per house, providing bricks to act as the new foundations. Robin was at pains to point out that the government is not insensitive to needs of the poor, that there are various schemes to improve housing and living conditions, but it is a never ending uphill struggle. However, he did admit that these improvements tend to occur just before the national or state elections and are likely to be followed by a barren period.

At least there were no 'slum' landlords here as in Calcutta and Bombay. These individuals exact 50 rupees a month from the slum dwellers not because they own the property but simply because they have sufficient political clout to prevent the authorities moving the inhabitants off government property – a refined protection racket. Here a labourer might expect to earn 15 rupees a day if he can find work, but another drain on finances has emerged, the rapid increase of alcoholism: very often no more than five rupees finds its way back to the household; the local brew, which was not recommended to me, costs three rupees a bottle. The small Christian community does its best to help, providing a weekly medical visitor and through its practical aid it has gradually become acceptable to the rest of the community. However, the Hindu community does not share the same concern for they believe if you are born poor, then that is your destiny and there is no obligation to change that situation. You must await your next reincarnation and if deserving you will return on a higher level. I'm bound to say that my grasp of the Hindu religion is not yet complete. I think I'd better return to the cricket.

At Nagpur the successful one-day combination was changed, which was just as well since the debutants, Moxon, Cowdrey and Agnew, were our main contributors – Moxon with a solid 70, Cowdrey a swashbuckling 46, which included an astonishing extra cover drive for six off Kapil. Agnew was our most effective bowler. The ground at Nagpur was reminiscent of Clarence Park, Weston-super-Mare, with ramshackle stands and a bumpy outfield; the pavilion, however, was far more luxurious. After five overs one of these makeshift stands collapsed like a breaking wave and seven rows of spectators disappeared from view. We were amazed – and relieved to hear that there were no fatalities. There was one other unusual incident. Allan Lamb damaged his left knee whilst batting and a runner (Fowler) was summoned. After a lengthy tactical discussion between the two of them, Allan hit the next ball wide of long-on and we were treated to the rare sight of both batsman and runner scampering two to the same end. We weren't sure whether to marvel at Lamb's enthusiasm or his complete lack of professionalism. Afterwards, whilst chuckling at his error he declared that he'd never batted with a runner before and he didn't intend to again.

We lost our 100 per cent one-day record as Gavaskar and Kapil Dev finally joined forces to add 76 for the Indian fifth wicket. Kapil struck some astonishing blows over the long-on boundary, whilst Sunil manipulated singles. It was interesting to watch them both; there appeared to be very little verbal communication but plenty of gesticulations as if they were demonstrating to the 15,000 crowd that there was a unity of purpose without necessarily admitting it to one another. When Kapil smashed a boundary Sunil would tap his bat in applause and then raise his glove as if to say 'keep calm'. If Kapil swung and missed, he would clench his fist or beat his thigh in self-recrimination. It all struck me as too theatrical to be completely genuine. Still the partnership prospered and England experienced its first hiccough for over a month. In the dressing room Gower demanded our attention for a few moments – 'We'd let ourselves down today, there had been an air of complacency, a lack of total commitment; let's get it right at Chandigarh and even more importantly at Kanpur'.

We now had two free days so all of us moved on to Agra and the Taj Mahal, except Mike Gatting, who had seen it before. Another 5 a.m. call was booked, but this time at our own volition: none of us regretted the decision as we witnessed the majesty of the Taj Mahal at sunrise. I tried in vain to describe the scene in my monthly letter to *The Cricketer*.

'Words fail to recapture . . . No. As the orange orb hovered above the hazy horizon, glistening, glimmering upon the massive marble dome of Mumtaz's mausoleum . . . No. It was jolly pretty.' Photographers from Murrell to Marks clicked away in an attempt to catch something of the Taj's splendour. It was a happy expedition as both press and players posed incessantly for cameras; everyone was anxious to record on film their presence in India in 1984/85, even Henri summoned Adrian Murrell to capture him and his wife staring dreamily at one another with the Taj in the background. As usual my photographic history of this tour will reflect three days out of 130.

By contrast Chandigarh is not a very uplifting place. After partition, Amritsar became the capital of the Indian Punjab, but since it was uncomfortably close to the Pakistan border it was decided to construct a totally new capital. The Indians are inordinately proud of Chandigarh but to us the town was dull and dismal. Between buildings there are long, ugly barren stretches of wasteland: no doubt the architect had intended verdant parks and colourful gardens but in India empty ground is doomed to dereliction. The architect was Le

Corbusier. For us the most notable feature was the Kapil Hotel, a gift to the former Indian captain following the 1983 World Cup victory. On the evening before the match the locals were treated to an extraordinary sight. Kapil and his wife had invited Sunil and wife to dinner there and they all sat down whilst the remainder of the restaurant looked on in disbelief. Sunil has been at pains to point out that there is no personal animosity between the two yet no-one is quite prepared to believe him. My sources have not revealed the content of the evening's conversation but I suggest that it touched upon the shortcomings of the Indian press rather more frequently than the final afternoon at Delhi.

After defeat at Nagpur, the final one-day match acquired greater significance. It was deemed important not to give the Indians any psychological advantage before the last Test so it was announced that the projected plan of playing Bruce French had been scrapped. Paul Downton was not particularly impressed by this decision, nor was Bruce and to me it seemed an unnecessary slight upon French's ability.

In the end Bruce did make his debut for England as the match was reduced to 15 overs per innings because of torrential overnight rain. For a while it seemed unlikely that we would have a game at all but it was a wise decision to play despite the drenched outfield, especially since the Punjab cricket authorities had spent over 200,000 rupees to prepare the ground for its first international match and the capacity 25,000 crowd had waited so patiently under bright sunshine. Our side was rearranged to suit the new conditions and I have to tell you that Marks was informed by the England captain that he had been selected purely for his batting. Someone, somewhere, must have turned in his grave.

The crowd's patience was rewarded with an exciting game of something. I'd be reluctant to call it cricket. For us Fowler, Gatting, Gower and Lamb biffed, banged and walloped to good effect but my debut as a pure batsman was shattered by Lamb's appalling running between the wickets; he banged (or was it biffed?) the ball to straight extra cover and started running so I reluctantly started running too and when Srikkanth's throw hit the stumps, I just kept running right to the boundary rope, whereupon I hurled the bat to the ground in disgust. I couldn't stop smiling though. It has always been a secret ambition of mine to sprint to the pavilion in such circumstances, although I hadn't planned to do it in an international match.

The Indians were required to score at eight an over and they couldn't quite manage it. Edmonds and Ellison, using all their one-day experience, fired the ball at the batsmen's feet, the fielders slithered around in various quagmires, Jon Agnew nonchalantly clung onto a skier to remove Kapil and Chris Cowdrey, summoned to bowl the last over in place of a wayward Gatting, ended with the impressive figures of 1-0-3-1, which prompted the headlines in the *Daily Telegraph* – 'Cowdrey saves England'. Later Chris admitted to being slightly flattered by the headline even though all six balls were jolly good ones. Still, it was a sweet victory for the only satisfaction to be gained from such a game is actually winning and 4–1 sounded much better than 3-2.

Throughout the one-day series the Indian papers focused upon the Englishmen's 'professionalism' and certainly our extra one-day experience helped as did winning the toss, for India have yet to beat England, batting first in a one-day game. However, we felt that we never really performed to our full potential. Only Mike Gatting at Poona played a major innings and some of the targets were achieved only after unnecessary alarms. The Indians, though strong in batting, were a remarkably thin bowling side. In most games we regarded Prabhakar, a very medium paced swing bowler, as the most obvious threat yet when we play Australia in Melbourne he is the sort of bowler that will be singled out as potential cannon fodder. There the challenge will be more severe and of different dimensions, the ball will arrive quicker and bounce more. Still I mustn't belittle our achievements too much. English success overseas is a rare commodity and it is grand to win the one-day series but people, quite rightly, will judge the tour upon the outcome of the Test series. We have just one hurdle left to clear.

INDIA v ENGLAND (THIRD ONE-DAY INTERNATIONAL)

Played at M. Chinnaswamy Stadium, Bangalore. January 20
Toss: ENGLAND ENGLAND won by 3 wickets

INDIA

*S. M. Gavaskar	c Gatting b Marks	40
K. Srikkanth	b Cowans	29
D. B. Vengsarkar	st Downton b Marks	23
Kapil Dev	c Gower b Marks	8
Yashpal Sharma	run out	8
R. J. Shastri	b Edmonds	33
M. Azharuddin	not out	47
†S. Viswanath	not out	6
R. S. Ghai		
A. Patel	did not bat	
T. A. Sekar		
Extras	(B4 LB6 W1)	11
Total	(6 wkts 46 Overs)	205

Fall of Wickets: 1–70, 2–70, 3–90, 4–108, 5–119, 6–135.
Bowling: Cowans 10–1–31–1; Foster 6–0–33–0; Ellison 6–0–25–0; Marks 10–1–35–3; Edmonds 10–0–44–1; Gatting 4–0–27–0.

ENGLAND

G. Fowler	run out	45
R. T. Robinson	c Viswanath b Kapil Dev	2
M. W. Gatting	run out	3
*D. I. Gower	b Shastri	38
A. J. Lamb	not out	59
V. J. Marks	c Gavaskar b Patel	17
†P. R. Downton	c Shastri b Kapil Dev	12
P. H. Edmonds	c Viswanath b Kapil Dev	7
R. M. Ellison	not out	1
N. A. Foster	did not bat	
N. G. Cowans		
Extras	(LB10 W7 NB5)	22
Total	(7 wkts 45 Overs)	206

Fall of Wickets: 1–15, 2–21, 3–91, 4–103, 5–144, 6–186, 7–204.
Bowling: Kapil Dev 10–0–38–3; Sekar 9–0–36–0; Patel 10–1–42–1; Ghai 4–0–37–0; Shastri 10–2–29–1; Yashpal 2–0–14–0.
Umpires: S. K. Das and S. V. Ramani.

INDIA v ENGLAND (FOURTH ONE-DAY INTERNATIONAL)

Played at V.C.A. Ground, Nagpur. January 23
Toss: INDIA INDIA won by 3 wickets

ENGLAND

G. Fowler	b Shastri	37
M. D. Moxon	c Srikkanth b Kapil Dev	70
M. W. Gatting	b Shastri	1
*D. I. Gower	c and b Shastri	11
A. J. Lamb	st Viswanath b Shastri	30
C. S. Cowdrey	not out	46
V. J. Marks	b Sekar	4
†P. R. Downton	c Rajput b Sekar	13
P. H. Edmonds	not out	8
J. P. Agnew N. G. Cowans	did not bat	
Extras	(B3 LB15 W1 NB1)	20
Total	(7 wkts 50 Overs)	240

Fall of Wickets: 1–70, 2–78, 3–100, 4–156, 5–176, 6–199, 7–221.
Bowling: Kapil Dev 10–1–12–1; Prabhakar 10–1–36–0; Sekar 10–0–50–2; Patel 10–1–51–0; Shastri 10–1–40–4.

INDIA

K. Srikkanth	b Cowans	6
L. S. Rajput	c Downton b Cowans	0
D. B. Vengsarkar	c Downton b Agnew	11
M. Azharuddin	b Cowdrey	47
*S. M. Gavaskar	b Agnew	52
Kapil Dev	c Gatting b Cowans	54
R. J. Shastri	not out	24
M. Prabhakar	b Agnew	4
†S. Viswanath	not out	23
A. Patel T. A. Sekar	did not bat	
Extras	(B3 LB14 W1 NB2)	20
Total	(7 wkts 47.4 Overs)	241

Fall of Wickets: 1–5, 2–11, 3–31, 4–90, 5–166, 6–197, 7–204.
Bowling: Cowans 10–0–44–3; Agnew 10–0–38–3; Marks 6–0–32–0; Edmonds 10–0–44–0; Cowdrey 7.4–0–52–1; Gatting 4–0–14–0.
Umpires: R. Mrithyunjayan and A. L. Narasimhan.

INDIA v ENGLAND (FIFTH ONE-DAY INTERNATIONAL)

Played at Sector 16 Stadium, Chandigarh. January 27

Toss: INDIA ENGLAND won by 7 runs

ENGLAND

G. Fowler	run out	17
M. W. Gatting	c Azharuddin b Sekar	31
*D. I. Gower	b Sekar	19
A. J. Lamb	not out	33
C. S. Cowdrey	c Rajput b Shastri	5
P. H. Edmonds	c Azharuddin b Sekar	5
V. J. Marks	run out	2
R. M. Ellison	not out	4
†B. N. French		
N. A. Foster	did not bat	
J. P. Agnew		
Extras	(LB5)	5
Total	(6 wkts 15 Overs)	121

Fall of Wickets: 1–31, 2–71, 3–74, 4–86, 5–93, 6–104.

Bowling: Kapil Dev 3–0–17–0; Prabhakar 3–0–26–0; C. Sharma 3–0–20–0; Sekar 3–0–23–3; Shastri 3–0–30–1.

INDIA

R. J. Shastri	run out	53
K. Srikkanth	run out	9
Kapil Dev	c Agnew b Edmonds	17
M. Azharuddin	c Gatting b Edmonds	10
Yashpal Sharma	b Cowdrey	6
*S. M. Gavaskar	not out	2
L. S. Rajput	not out	1
M. Prabhakar		
†S. Viswanath	did not bat	
C. Sharma		
T. A. Sekar		
Extras	(LB4 W12)	16
Total	(5 wkts 15 Overs)	114

Fall of Wickets: 1–22, 2–49, 3–83, 4–111, 5–112.

Bowling: Agnew 3–0–23–0; Foster 3–0–17–0; Ellison 3–0–20–0; Edmonds 3–0–20–2; Gatting 2–0–27–0; Cowdrey 1–0–3–1.

Umpires: A. Nagaraja Rao and Ram Babu.

13
Kanpur

Not many tourists go to Kanpur. Even though it has a population of 1,500,000 it occupies no more than an inch and a half of my tattered guidebook. I can tell you that during the 1857 mutiny Sir Hugh Wheeler defended it, the Indians surrounded it, and Sir Hugh finally surrendered it only to have his entire party massacred. (I declined to mention this at the team meeting lest it undermine the morale of David Gower's men.) It also has a large and modern zoo and I presume that this is a reference to the spacious Hotel Meghdoot, where we were billeted for a week.

Despite reports of especially stringent security arrangements our hotel lobby was forever crowded with onlookers eager to snatch a glimpse, an autograph or a photo of a Test cricketer. I can only assume that security guards at Kanpur are unusually virile and have remarkably large families. One evening I pottered into the hotel bar, which was deserted apart from a group of English journalists, no doubt discussing the use of the extended simile in modern prose. Within minutes the room was crammed with cameras, pens, paper and jostling, smiling Indians; someone had spotted the advent of this English cricketer even if no-one knew his 'good name'. Now whenever I'm accosted by admiring Indians who are not sure of my identity I foolishly invite them to guess it. This inevitably depresses me since the response is always the same: 'Pocock', now nearing his 39th birthday, followed by 'Edmonds', a mere 33. On this occasion I was rescued by Graham Morris, who redirected part of the avalanche towards himself by declaring that he was Norman Cowans. Quietly I tiptoed to bed looking forward to the time when this partial anonymity became complete.

By now you may be a trifle weary of reading about the appearance of distant strips of Indian soil but the nature of the wicket for the final Test did dominate our thoughts. There were two conflicting rumours about the pitch. The first was that Gavaskar, after India's defeat at Madras, had ordered a pitch that would assist the spinners and would not last five days; the second, less substantiated, was that the groundsman was a cousin of a former Indian opening batsman, who had been dropped by Gavaskar after a solitary international appearance and that for this reason the 'expert pitchmaker' had no intention of preparing anything other than the traditional Kanpur shirtfront. We naturally preferred to believe the latter. Anyway we all stared at the wicket for an inordinately long period of time; certainly there were a few cracks but the surrounding soil did not appear to be as mobile as in Delhi. Especially after the misreading of that Delhi wicket no-one was prepared to be dogmatic about this one's behaviour and all we knew was that we wanted to win the toss and bat for two days, thereby making the match and the series safe as soon as possible. However for the fourth consecutive time Gavaskar won the toss and, having strangely included an extra batsman, Malhotra, instead of an opening bowler, he naturally chose to bat.

The match was certainly a more absorbing draw than the Third Test at Calcutta if only because the outcome of the series depended upon the result. As usual batsmen will recall the Kanpur wicket with more affection than the bowlers; Kapil, belatedly discovering something of his old sparkle, was the game's highest wicket taker with four but there was scant encouragement for spinners or seamers. For India Srikkanth was Srikkanth, flirting outside the off stump, lofting drives over mid-off and treating subtle English off-spinners with unwarranted disdain again and with Azharuddin he added 150 in just 38 overs. Srikkanth always looks as if he might miscue at any time, but Azharuddin doesn't. As he shuffles out to the wicket, his lean, wiry frame slightly hunched, he is not an awesome sight. When Richards or Gatting enter an arena their intentions are clear: Richards is so aloof, so arrogant in appearance that he can intimidate a bowler before he takes strike; Gatting bustles out like a mini-Botham, swinging his bat in the widest possible arc, obviously intent on more than survival. Azhar looks a little embarrassed, like a precocious schoolboy playing his first match in adult company. If he cracks a boundary his eyes are more likely to focus upon his shoe laces than the humbled bowler; there are no external signs that he intends to dominate the bowlers and at the moment he doesn't appear to need this psychological advantage. His century at Kanpur created a new record – he became the first cricketer to score a century in each of his first three Tests – and Rajiv Gandhi, no less, was quick to congratulate him. At Kanpur he played exceptionally well, yet I think his previous two hundreds were more meritorious. At Calcutta he had shown the world and, in particular his captain, that he possessed an excellent temperament.

'Calcutta is not the easiest place to make your debut,' explained Sunil. 'For a start there are 80,000 people watching your every move and the Bengalis are far more emotionally volatile than anywhere else. So failure there is a massive setback and to have overcome that meant that his temperament was OK. After that it was a question of whether his technique would stand up and he's proven without doubt that on good wickets it does. The next test will be playing in England and against the West Indies, but I think he will be able to adjust.'

Gavaskar regards Azhar as a typical southern Indian: 'There, if you have noticed, the people tend to be more gentle, more polite, and more humble about their achievements.'

At Madras in the second innings it was the Indian team who were under pressure rather than himself. Arriving at the crease with the score on 22-3 he responded with a delightfully uninhibited innings, which, for a while, threatened to halt England's victory march. At Kanpur, however, there were no special internal or external crises so I can simply describe his knock as 'just another Azharuddin century'. I shall follow his career with interest.

Vengsarkar, batting at number five and obviously happier against the older ball, also scored a century, which nearly doubled his tally for the series. It was an accomplished innings, which may mask his earlier failures from future cricket statisticians. As the Indian total passed 500 with Kapil and Shastri opening their shoulders, we could at least take solace from the fact that the pitch showed no signs of misbehaving; barring a disaster of Ahmedabad proportions we knew that we should be able to make the game safe. When Gavaskar declared on the third morning our immediate target was 354, which would save the follow-on; our openers gave us a perfect start; Fowler was more restrained than at Madras whereas 'Old Man Robbo just keeps batting along', calm, controlled and delightfully predictable. A perfect day was marred only by Fowler's dismissal half an hour before stumps but not before England had accumulated 156. The success of England's opening pair has been a major factor in our ascendancy in this series; compare the opening partnerships of the two sides:

For England: 46, 3, 15, 41, 71, 178, 156.

For India: 47, 5, 3, 12, 28, 17, 7, 9, 2.

By the middle of the fourth day England were 276-3 with Gatting and Gower comfortably established at the crease and saving the follow-on seemed to be little more than a formality. Twenty minutes later with the score at 286–6 it had become a good each-way bet. The tiny off-spinner, Gopal Sharma, on his debut for India captured all three wickets; he had been lucky enough to have the ball in his hand when we collapsed at Ahmedabad and no doubt the Indian selectors had hoped that his mere presence would resurrect the memories of last November's humiliation. For twenty minutes he achieved this as Gatting, Cowdrey and Downton departed in quick succession; only Gower and Edmonds of the recognised batsmen remained (though I know that Neil Foster will now take umbrage if he reads this) and maybe it was fitting that these two should guide us to safety. Gower at the end of an arduous tour, during which he has been haunted by poor form, dubious umpiring decisions and a recent concern about his eyesight, had nonetheless refused to let these setbacks affect his demeanour or his captaincy whilst none of the bowlers had striven harder or bowled more overs than Phil Emonds – Gower's old protégé. For three and a half months both had extended themselves to the full without obvious rewards and now they were determined that our hard-won advantage should not be frittered away on the penultimate day of the series.

Once the follow-on had been averted the game was dead, even though there were some desperate Indian attempts to resurrect it on the final day. In their second innings they smashed 97 from 14 overs; Azharuddin scored another 50 and I'm sure that he would have reached a fourth century if the situation had not demanded a declaration. Gavaskar set us a target of 233 in 43 overs, which was politely ignored. Gower opened instead of Fowler, whose stomach was disordered again, and after Robinson had retired with contact lens problems England's captain and vice-captain sedately took us to stumps, bringing the series to a close with a wonderful whimper. Gower left the field in the knowledge that he now joined Greig and Jardine as the only English captains to win a series on Indian soil and neither of these had had to fight back from being 1-0 down. At first glance this may seem to be the only thing that these three English captains have in common. After careful deliberation I've reached the same conclusion; Gower bats left-handed, is not desperately single-minded and though successful in Australia, has never yet caused the Australian Cricket Board to convene in frenzied debate. No doubt the erudite or obtuse amongst you will find the link.

Having unbuckled his pads and swallowed a bottle of Blue Diamond beer he led his side back onto the field for the presentations. He collected a handsome trophy, was hoisted onto Gatting's ample shoulders, whereupon he dropped it on Gatting's head; fortunately the trophy survived and everyone was happy. After this he conducted one of the easiest press conferences of his life before passing a forlorn Gavaskar on his way to one of his least comfortable. In the evening a few champagne bottles were popped (we only had a few) but Kanpur is not ideally suited to wild celebrations so most of the players retired to the top floor snooker room, where I imagine that the press corps were completely humiliated, yet again.

I had arranged to meet with Sunil in his hotel room. Again the 'Indian' corridor was overrun with security guards plus relatives, hotel porters plus relatives, waiters plus relatives – mayhem. I was swiftly ushered into his room by his wife and I found him giving an interview to two journalists. Sunil is very wary of the Indian press, especially after the Kapil Affair and the Calcutta Test, but he had decided to speak to two of the more trustworthy scribes, who would not distort his statements. All the while the phone or the doorbell was ringing. He finally invited me back to his in-laws' house in Kanpur, a rare haven for the Gavaskars in India. His lack of privacy surpasses anything that a British sportsman has to endure. Sunil and Pammie, his wife, have not been out shopping together for years and even when they held a small drinks party in their Kanpur garden, the balconies and trees of the neighbouring households were lined with spectators. Soon after I arrived at the family home two bashful, awestruck ten year olds were ushered into the living room for an autograph and a friendly word. Despite the disappointments of the day, the constant attention from the media and elsewhere, he seemed remarkably relaxed as he indulged in a rare glass of white wine. At the dinner table Pammie guided me through the various Indian concoctions, which I naturally assaulted with a knife and fork whilst Sunil, despite his frequent exposures to the ways of the west, scooped it down with nan bread and his fingers. We talked a little about the series just ended.

If nothing else, this had been a harmonious tour – at least on the field; there had been no ugly incidents and the players had ended the season as friends. This had stemmed from a healthy relationship between the two captains, which Sunil regards as being vital in a Test series: 'Once the captains have a fair respect for each other, I think the rest of the team follows. If a captain comes back to the dressing room and starts having a go at his opposite number, that obviously affects the attitude of his side. I got along with Keith Fletcher in 1981/2 but we couldn't really share a joke together whereas with David right from the time we walked out to toss we used to pull each other's legs.' Neither Gavaskar nor Gower can be described as dour, blinkered professionals; Sunil has mellowed over the years; he strives as hard, perhaps harder for success as the next man but sometimes the fates will not permit it and that sad state of affairs is now readily accepted. Gower has been described as 'laid back' from the moment Ray Illingworth first told him to buckle up his pads for Leicestershire ten years ago. Scoring runs and winning cricket matches is important, but not all important. I'm sure both would have exasperated Bill Shankly – 'Football is not a matter of life and death – it's far more important than that'.

So Sunil naturally warmed to Gower and when I tried to provoke a few criticisms of England's captain on tour he was reluctant to oblige: 'It's much too easy to criticise a captain especially with hindsight,' he said, with feeling. He wasn't very interested in minor technicalities such as whether Cowans should have bowled more on the fourth afternoon at Delhi; rather he concentrated on the man. 'He looks to be an innately good human being and therefore bound to gain respect from his players. After the Delhi Test Pammie said to me "I'm sorry you lost but I'm feeling so much happier seeing David Gower smile". She had been in England during the 1984 season and had observed that "he looked so worried on TV, always frowning and he was the same in Bombay". She had seen me win some matches but that was David's first win as captain; now, if the opposition captain's wife feels that way I'm sure that within the team there must be a lot of goodwill towards him.' I wonder whether Mrs Border will be similarly delighted if England win the First Test next summer.

The cricket had been more interesting than in 1981/2; the 80 overs a day regulation had helped and Sunil, despite being party to the tedium of 81/2, advocated a 6-hour day and a minimum of 90 overs. Many more shots had been played, which could be attributable to the advent of concentrated one-day cricket in India, and too much cricket against the West Indies; suddenly seeing the ball landing in the batsman's half of the wicket had excited the Indians despite their implacable reputation. The most successful batsmen, Gatting and Azharuddin, were naturally aggressive players, but in 1981/2 three of the principal runscorers were obdurate, conscientious types, who were not attractive to watch – Boycott and Tavare for England and he added with a twinkle in his eye 'Gavaskar for India'. The contest between Gatting and Siva had been fascinating to watch even if it became a little one-sided by the end, for Siva's last four Test wickets cost a hundred runs each. Although Siva was declared man of the series his international future is not yet assured. Sunil explained his team mate's limitations:

'On a slightly helpful wicket he is a dificult proposition because he bowls the ball with a flat trajectory. When he came into the Indian squad two years ago he had a lovely loop, which invited the batsman to step down the track. Since then he has played a lot of domestic one-day cricket and he has become flatter – not such an attacking bowler. At Bombay the wicket assisted him and that being your first serious encounter with him he was successful. Thereafter the wickets were better and at Madras, where at least the ball bounced, he was under pressure from his home crowd and tried to do too many things.'

We agreed that this England side could not match Fletcher's tourists man for man, which left us a little puzzled by England's victory. We could pinpoint the reasons for India's defeat relatively easily, but it was more difficult to explain them. There was not one opening partnership of any substance and in the middle order they missed the presence of Vishwanath, of whom Sunil speaks as admiringly as Somerset players do of Richards. As a bowler Kapil Dev was no longer the attacking force of 1981/2 – 'When he was injury free, he was much sharper and he made the ball swing consistently' and once Siva was mastered, there was no-one to provide the mesmeric qualities of Dilip Doshi, who took 22 wickets at an average of 21 in 1981/2.

This was a less disciplined Indian side: 'Whatever strategy we had in 1981 we stuck to it; but this summer pre-match resolutions often went overboard. For instance, I always stressed the importance of batting for four or five sessions in the first innings, yet at Madras we were dismissed in four and a half hours.'

Maybe too many of this experienced Indian side were jaded by an excess of Test cricket in recent years; they had lost that vital competitive edge whereas almost every member of the touring party had something to prove. Apart from Gower, who was still on trial as captain, and Lamb, none of the sixteen were firmly established at the beginning of the tour. For the Indians it was Siva, Azharuddin and Amarnath, who had recently been omitted from the squad, who made the greatest impact. Admittedly Shastri, 'a 30 year head on 20 year old shoulders', has blossomed into a batsman of international stature, but this has coincided with a decline in his bowling. The old hands, Kirmani as a keeper, Kapil, Vengsarkar and Gavaskar himself, with almost 300 Test caps between them, would not have been content with their performances.

'There was a certain amount of staleness in some of us; we went about our jobs mechanically or from memory rather than approaching the games in a fresh enthusiastic manner.'

'And complacency after England's U25 defeat and the Bombay Test?'

'Yes. Look at the shots we played on the first day at Delhi; some were terrible even by one-day standards. If you had not won at Delhi, I'm sure the series would have taken a different course. That match really rejuvenated your side whereas it completely shattered the Indian team; our morale was severely damaged by its aftermath. Then we desperately needed to win the one-day match at Cuttack on the eve of the Calcutta Test, but we lost that as well.'

We agreed that the whole series hinged on the final afternoon at Delhi when I combated the spin of Gifford and French in the nets far more effectively than the Indian middle order batsmen dealt with Edmonds and Pocock. That startling collapse undermined the confidence of the Indian team for the rest of the series. I tried to take our conversation back to that afternoon but Sunil, with a hint of mischief, groaned: 'Please don't remind me of it'. So being more unctious than Parkinson, Harty and Wogan put together, I didn't.

Sunil himself had never endured such a long run of failures as an international batsman. How had he coped with this unusual experience?

'I used to be very uptight about being successful until the 1980/1 season when I went to Australia. Perhaps playing for Somerset (in 1980) had an effect. There was one Benson and Hedges match against Middlesex, which we lost by one run (Sunil scored a magnificent 123). If it had been for Bombay or India, that result would have made me sit down for the whole evening brooding. But over there I saw a different attitude – that this is still a game; winning or losing does not always mean everything. Even after a close loss we could still be dispassionate about the game. So when I'd had a bad series against Australia and New Zealand and I was a failure, I came back and found that my friends were still the same; nobody turned their backs on me and so I said "Why was I getting so worked up about being successful all this time?" That was the turning point in my attitude towards cricket.'

This strikes me as a mature and enlightened approach towards cricket, though I wonder whether Sunil would have rewritten the record books so frequently if he had adopted this outlook earlier in his career.

Despite the disappointments of the summer, Sunil was excited by the one-day competition in Australia. 'I really enjoy one-day cricket. Just because I have been the old school opening batsman, who has been taught to take the shine off the ball and not to play too many aggressive shots, people think I hate it, but I don't.' I was surprised by such enthusiasm. 'The press builds an image of you; even if you turn out to be different, the press do not like to be proved wrong so they perpetuate that image regardless of the reality and it continues until the end of your career.'

Sunil will probably relinquish the captaincy after the Australian trip, but he has not ruled out the possibility of touring England once more as a player. If he does I'm sure he'll enjoy himself; his sense of humour and his cricket will become even more mischievous (though I'll be disappointed if he starts reverse lapping my off-spinners) and he may even enjoy the luxury of taking his wife shopping – it's a strange world, where that becomes a luxury. I left around midnight as the Gavaskars, anxious not to disappoint some long-standing acquaintances, set off a little wearily for a drinks party on the other side of Kanpur.

Our final internal flight took us back to Delhi for two days of packing and shopping – carpets and jewellery for the single or rich, leather jackets for the poor marrieds; my jacket fitted perfectly. We paid a final visit to the faithful British High Commission bar, a recurring landmark in our progress through India. Back in November we had crept in there, uncertain about our future, suspicious of India and Indians, and bemused by events around us. In December one or two of us were still bemused after the final day's play of the Second Test – we had enjoyed John Smith's on that evening. Now we returned, having surpassed everyone's expectations, grateful that the Delhi diplomats had advised us to continue with the tour.

A team meeting was summoned, where presents and farewells were delivered to two very important people whom I'm ashamed to admit have hardly had a mention so far. Charlie Pinto, our 'courier' from Trade Wings of Bombay, was responsible for transporting the party around India; he ensured that buses arrived at the hotel to take us to the ground, the receptions and the airport, where he would placate any perplexed official as he guided us to the VIP lounge – if there was one. With cheerful, calm efficiency he unravelled the intricacies of our wives' airline tickets and organised their internal travel as well as our own. The usual problems – 'Charlie, my wife was coming to Delhi and flying to Gauhati, now she's arriving at Bombay and wants to come straight to Calcutta, can you arrange that?' – were greeted with a smile and the words 'No problem'. In India this response can often mean 'I more or less understand what you want and if I've got time I'll try to do something about it' but with Charlie 'No problem' meant 'No problem'. In fact our journeys throughout India were relatively trouble free. Apart from our coach drive to Poona, we travelled exclusively by air and I can recall only two significant delays at airports. Constant packing and travelling is obviously a bore but we became almost anaesthetised to it. Half a dozen Walkman cassette recorders appear – Henri listens to classical music, Flash to reggae – whilst in Botham's absence, Gatting's Super wuffer dominates the back of the coach and regularly pumps out Phil Collins, Elton John and Tina Turner. Week-old *Daily Telegraph* crosswords may be perused by Cowdrey and Marks and probably completed by Gower; once the crossword is finished – or abandoned – we'll check on Michael Carey's cricket report, followed by the football results; then we'll briefly examine the latest situation in the miners' strike and if after all that we're either depressed or homesick, we'll turn to the weather reports.

Our other indispensable companion was Govind, the baggage man, who has been carting English cricket cases around India since the 1950s – and he hasn't lost one yet. We had too much luggage for the internal flights to bear so Govind would depart the day before us by truck or train to our next destination. Often he, or one of his sons, would sleep in the dressing room to guard our kit at the more obscure venues. At lunch and tea intervals he would dispense corned beef, baked beans or sandwiches with a gracious smile. Nothing was too much trouble for him – another cup of tea, some whitener, a plane for a heavy bat – and at Rajkot he acted as both interpreter and butler as he organised the non-English speaking hotel staff to deliver our breakfast. He even managed to endure the constant playful banter of Allan Lamb for three and a half months without a trace of irritation. Truly the salt of the earth and I fancy he was a little watery-eyed on our departure.

We also bade a reluctant farewell to Bruce French and Pat Pocock; the rules of the Australian competition limited each squad to fourteen and the predictions of September were fulfilled when these two were omitted. Bruce French, despite limited opportunities, had performed excellently behind the stumps and off the field he had proved to be the ideal tourist, an essential quality for reserve wicket-keepers. He can return home happy in the knowledge that he has represented England, albeit in a 15-over match, that he's seen Everest and that he helped save the life of an Indian maiden, not a bad combination and certainly an unusual one. By the time we reach Melbourne he'll have disappeared into the Nottinghamshire country-side to an old barn, which he and his wife are renovating together. Maybe this long-term project has helped him to develop the patience that enabled him to remain cheerful and sane throughout three and a half months during which he played fifteen days' cricket.

Pat Pocock enjoyed his tour but then he would enjoy watching a tap drip providing he had someone to talk to. His figures in the Test matches may not be that impressive yet at Delhi his bowling was absolutely crucial to our victory and everywhere else his boundless enthusiasm and sharp cricket brain were equally vital. Just before the Madras Test he noticed that Graeme Fowler's batting grip had altered slightly; he mentioned this to Graeme, who made the necesssary adjustment, and prospered. After a long winter some of us may feel a little jaded and lukewarm about running up to bowl into an icy wind on 27 April, but I'm sure Pat won't. We may even miss his jokes, though I think we know most of them by now.

Finally the captain commented upon the excellent team spirit over the last three and a half months, though I'm never sure whether this nebulous quality causes victories or is a consequence of them, and he thanked everyone sincerely for their co-operation and support throughout the tour. On this occasion his speech was no formality; he really meant it and it showed.

INDIA v ENGLAND (FIFTH TEST MATCH)

Played at Green Park, Kanpur. January 31, February 1, 3, 4, 5
Toss: INDIA Match Drawn

INDIA

*S. M. Gavaskar	b Cowans	9		
K. Srikkanth	c Downton b Foster	84	not out	41
M. Azharuddin	c sub (R. M. Ellison) b Cowdrey	122	not out	54
M. Amarnath	b Cowans	15		
D. B. Vengsarkar	c Downton b Foster	137		
A. Malhotra	lbw b Pocock	27		
R. J. Shastri	b Edmonds	59	(1) run out	2
Kapil Dev	c Gower b Foster	42		
†S. M. H. Kirmani	not out	16		
L. Sivaramakrishnan	not out	16		
G. Sharma	did not bat			
Extras	(B9 LB12 W5)	26		
Total	(8 wkts dec)	553	(1 wkt dec)	97

Fall of Wickets:
1st Innings: 1–19, 2–169, 3–209, 4–277, 5–362, 6–457, 7–511, 8–533.
2nd Innings: 1–2.

Bowling:
1st Innings: Cowans 36–9–115–2; Foster 36–8–123–3; Pocock 24–2–79–1; Edmonds 48–16–112–1; Cowdrey 21–1–103–1.
2nd Innings: Cowans 7–0–51–0; Cowdrey 5–0–39–0; Gatting 1–0–7–0.

ENGLAND

G. Fowler	c Kirmani b Shastri	69		
R. T. Robinson	lbw b Kapil Dev	96	retired hurt	16
M. W. Gatting	c and b Sharma	62	not out	41
A. J. Lamb	c Srikkanth b Shastri	13		
*D. I. Gower	lbw b Shastri	78	(1) not out	32
C. S. Cowdrey	c Kirmani b Sharma	1		
†P. R. Downton	b Sharma	1		
P. H. Edmonds	lbw b Kapil Dev	49		
N. A. Foster	c Kirmani b Kapil Dev	8		
P. I. Pocock	not out	4		
N. G. Cowans	b Kapil Dev	9		
Extras	(B10 LB17)	27	(LB2)	2
Total		417	(no wkt)	91

Fall of Wickets:
1st Innings: 1–156, 2–196, 3–222, 4–276, 5–278, 6–286, 7–386, 8–402, 9–404, 10–417.

Bowling:
1st Innings: Kapil Dev 36.5–7–81–4; Amarnath 4–1–6–0; Sharma 60–16–115–3; Sivaramakrishnan 54–11–133–0; Shastri 32–13–52–3; Malhotra 2–0–3–0.
2nd Innings: Kapil Dev 5–0–19–0; Shastri 7–2–12–0; Sharma 11–4–17–0; Sivaramakrishnan 10–2–22–0; Srikkanth 2–0–11–0; Azharuddin 1–0–8–0.

Umpires: V. K. Ramaswamy and P. D. Reporter.

14
Australia

If I can equate the tour of India to the Greeks' famous triumph over the Persians in 490 BC and 480 BC, then our month in Australia recalls the disastrous Sicilian Expedition of 415 BC. I realise that this parallel may not be too precise or familiar, but I have a grim determination to put my distant classical education to use before I forget it all and time is running out.

As you probably know at the beginning of the fifth century BC a massive Persian force descended upon Greece under the command of Xerxes (maybe not an exact replica of Gavaskar), intent upon conquest. However the citizens of the various Greek states united under Themistocles and though completely outnumbered they managed to thwart and defeat the Persians, thereby defying the odds and, I suspect, surprising themselves. In the same way (well, almost) twenty pale Englishmen against 700 million Indians had contrived a victory equally unexpected.

By 415 BC Athens had become a powerful empire and decided to embark upon an ambitious expedition to a distant, prosperous island, Sicily. However the expedition, which took place at the end of the long, gruelling Peloponnesian War, was ill-fated and hampered by crises of leadership. There were indeed two disastrous night battles on the island and after a long campaign the Athenian forces were clobbered by all and sundry before limping back to Athens in dribs and drabs. So if anyone wants to find out what really happened in Australia, I suggest you buy a copy of Thucydides. I now have a clear mental picture of Donald Carr, my gracious TCCB censor, thumbing through the text, my only uncertainty being whether he is using the Penguin translation or not.

Sydney is different to Delhi or Bombay or Calcutta. There is no smog, no dust and you can see for miles: colours are crisper, wine is twenty times cheaper and the cheese is not only reliable, but tasty. It was strange to experience clean pavements, ordered hooter-free traffic jams, telephone operators who understood and waiters who didn't ask for autographs and passes. For three days we simply wallowed in the luxury of it all. David Gower disappeared to Tasmania to reunite with his old Leicestershire colleague, Brian Davison; Mike Gatting, who had dominated grade cricket here for a couple of years, had countless reunions as did former Sydney grade cricketers Cowdrey and Agnew. I shared a meal with Peter Roebuck, who teaches here, and received a potted version of the Australian summer: the devastation caused by Malcolm Marshall, the desolation of Kim Hughes and the mini-resurgence of the Australian side following their draw at Adelaide and their convincing spin-inspired victory in the final Test when Clive Lloyd strangely elected to field first on a turning Sydney wicket.

We also discussed the interminable triangular World Series competition, which was now grinding to a conclusion. The West Indies had won each of their ten qualifying games, the Australians four and the Sri Lankans one. All three sides were exhausted by a surfeit of one-day cricket, yet the competition was finally brought to life when Australia, having won the first final at Sydney scored 272 from their 50 overs in the second at Melbourne. In a thrilling climax Jeff Dujon and Gus Logie took the West Indies to victory and experienced campaigners such as Viv Richards, Michael Holding and Clive Lloyd himself rushed from the dressing room to embrace the architects of victory. The following day the banner headlines on the sports pages came from the lips of Gus Logie, 'We did it for you, skip'. Clive Lloyd, who has just been honoured with the Order of Australia, may have an abundance of talent at his disposal but the devotion and respect that he engenders from his side has ensured that they continue to perform to their ability when less motivated teams would wilt under the sheer volume of cricket. Two weeks later every team attended a dinner in Clive's honour where the Prime Minister made a further presentation to cricket's longest serving captain. Throughout the evening Bob Hawke was completely overshadowed by Clive's presence – what is more he didn't even seem to mind. Inevitably the third and decisive final in Sydney was comfortably won by the West Indies.

Pete and I decided that the Australian Cricket Board were doing cricket, the players, maybe even the spectators, a disservice by insisting on such a long drawn out one-day competition at the end of a gruelling Test series. The entrepreneurs of PBL Marketing obviously hold a different view. Later in the tour after articles in the press from two contrasting Cantabs, Henry Blofeld and Roebuck himself, about cricket's overkill, the wise editor of *The Cricketer*, Christopher Martin Jenkins, suggested that the players as well as the administrators should shoulder some of the blame for the current state of affairs; the players as a body should refuse to adhere to the demands made upon them. I was surprised to hear such an anarchic view from such an established establishment quarter. Certainly more consultation should be welcomed but in the end the administrators should administrate and the players should be left to concentrate on playing, rather than leading a revolution to reform the game, thereby undermining their futures as they risk being labelled troublemakers, rebels or just 'fairly nice chaps'.

Our thoughts naturally turned to Somerset. We were alarmed by the proximity of April and the emergence of the 1985 fixture list in *The Cricketer*. Within seven weeks we would be trundling around the boundary of the County Ground at Taunton, delving into cupboards for extra sweaters to take to the windswept Parks on 20 April and soon afterwards desperately searching for our first Championship run or wicket against Nottinghamshire, consoled only by the fact that Richard Hadlee would still be in the West Indies – gulp, so would Viv and Joel. For the last two years February has been a time when the attractions of a premature retirement loom largest. After four months in an undiluted cricket environment, utterly rootless and shunted from one pristine hotel room to another, the prospect (if there is one) of a really boring home-based 9 to 5 job isn't too bad. But don't fret, Both, come 20 April I'll be champing at the bit and raring to go – I think.

Before flying down to Melbourne we had one net practice at the Sydney Cricket Ground and a match against a Sydney District XI at the University of New South Wales. There we scrambled a mere 149 in 50 overs, but thanks to a steady bowling performance and Australian panic at the thought of such an historic victory, we won by four runs. I clung on to quite a difficult caught-and-bowled chance, which prompted Graeme Fowler to try to embrace me. I swiftly pushed him aside exhorting him through my teeth not to look so surprised. If nothing else, this match proved that any complacency was totally unwarranted.

We had triumphed in India not because we were a great side, but because we had played to the limits of our potential; anything less and we were a very ordinary side indeed; the West Indies might be able to cakewalk some games at half-throttle, but we couldn't. Our performance must have rung a few alarm bells as we practised for four hours on the day before our confrontation with Australia on 17 February, two hours in the afternoon, two under the lights.

The state of Victoria, which was celebrating its 150th anniversary in every imaginable way, was buzzing with anticipation at the prospect of this match. The unveiling of the lights and the presence of the arch enemy, England, ensured that the vast Melbourne arena was sold out. It was clearly going to be a special occasion and it took an age to arrive. From our hotel room 100 yards from the ground, the gleaming white towers which held a massive triangle of bulbs were easily visible, a constant reminder of the trials to come. The more squeamish amongst us could be forgiven for waking from a restless sleep screaming in Hitchcock style, 'The lights, the lights' as they hovered there outside our windows, unforgiving, uncaring, waiting for us. I exaggerate a bit; even when my arm ball refuses to swing and my cover drive doesn't even make it to third man, I manage to sleep at night. None the less we were all a little nervous.

The opening of 'The Greatest Show on Earth' was full of pomp and ceremony. The teams paraded around the arena Olympic style, smiling and waving with studied innocence at the spectators in Bay 13, who responded with their customary stream of abuse. It is important for an Australian sitting in the cheaper seats of the MCG to hurl abuse effectively at an English tourist for then he is a man and entirely acceptable to his colleagues. Finally we were ushered to our allotted spots around the podium erected at the members' end of the ground. Ray Steele, the president of the Victorian Cricket Association, ascended and introduced the state's premier, John Cain. Mr Cain tried to make a speech but was quickly overwhelmed by chants of 'boring, boring'. Finally he descended, whilst trying to convey the impression like a good politician that 'that went pretty well, I think'. Up stepped Bob Hawke, a better politician or at least a more experienced one since within thirty seconds he had described the Victorians as 'the most knowledgeable and discerning cricket public in the world', which won him a few moments of silence. However the validity of that statement was later questioned with some vehemence by Jon Agnew after he had been repeatedly flashed at by one spectator in Bay 13, whilst fielding at third man. Mr

Hawke swiftly declared the competition to be opened, whereupon 'Waltzing Matilda' and 'Advance Australia Fair' was hammered out by the brass band. It amazes me how much time the Australians spend convincing themselves how lucky they are to be where they are – it should be perfectly obvious. There is a fervent nationalism, maybe stemming from TV advertising, which has manifested itself in events such as the 1982 Commonwealth Games in Brisbane and which, to the outsider, verges upon the unhealthy. Next Mr Hawke tossed a specially minted gold coin in front of the two captains and David Gower, a little suspicious of the lights' effectiveness, decided to bat.

The selection of the eleven for this game had caused considerable speculation amongst the touring party; not many of us got it right. In the end the selectors gambled upon opening the batting with Paul Downton thereby enabling Chris Cowdrey to play, giving us more cover in the bowling department and a potential sting in the middle order, his powers of improvisation back in Nagpur having made a vivid impression on us all. More surprisingly Jon Agnew was preferred to Neil Foster, the hero of Madras; I'm not sure why.

The decision to open with Downton was justified when he and Fowler added 61 for the first wicket, whereupon three wickets fell for 16 runs. Lamb, the only Englishman to play with his normal fluency, and Gatting restored the innings with a sensible partnership of 82 and a total around 250 seemed possible; however another three wickets fell in quick succession, this time for just 7 runs. Henri and I edged the score towards 200 but the sudden collapse had rendered any startling acceleration in the run rate unlikely. The Australians were impressive in the field, displaying their usual fierce commitment but you could tell that their bowlers were exhausted. They bowled with excellent control but no real pace. At the end of a long, demanding summer the strains upon their bodies and minds were obvious, but they refused to give in to them; the capture of an English wicket was greeted with relief rather than exultation.

Our final total of 214 from 49 overs was disappointing after such a good start but it gave us a chance and with Australia being reduced to 58 for 3, having lost three wickets for just one run, it seemed like a good chance. Richard Ellison, whose excellent opening spell gave him figures of 7–4–10–1, accounted for Wessels thanks to a superlative diving catch at slip by Gatting. Then Kim Hughes' turbulent summer reached a new nadir when he was run out for a duck and one run later Allan Border swept my first ball into the hands of Norman Cowans at deep backward square leg. So Australia's hopes now rested upon their two most inexperienced batsmen, Robbie Kerr from Queensland and Dean Jones from Victoria; they responded to the crisis in a typically brash and uninhibited manner with Jones, in particular, going for his shots.

As the stand developed I was conscious of an eerie atmosphere under the lights. With 85,000 present it was obviously noisy, yet in the middle against this distant backcloth of constant jeering and cheering, there was a strange silence. I could hear none of the usual bellows of encouragement from Downton and Gatting as they were drowned by the volume of the background noise. So each player was operating in a little world of his own, almost oblivious to his team-mates unless they were within a couple of yards. Edmonds' world was bubbling over with aggression and excitement at the big occasion. Once fielding at square leg he advanced with such abandon that he ended up no more than seven feet from the bat. When bowling he yelled abuse at erring fieldsmen – fortunately we couldn't hear him – and for a while he tormented the two youngsters, yet gradually the partnership prospered. Gower switched his bowlers around – maybe he could have tried Cowdrey as well – but it made no difference and an unbeaten stand of 157 ensured a decisive Australian victory.

Afterwards the Australians came into our dressing room accompanied by cans of XXXX lager; this is common practice over here. After spending eight hours desperately trying to outstrip each other, we sit down, drink lager and laugh together. Not everyone can adjust to this situation, some like Chris Tavare and Alan Knott prefer to keep their distance from the opposition, whereas Allan Lamb and David Gower are guaranteed to stay. On this occasion they were joined by Chris Cowdrey and Richard Ellison, who lingered with their recent Kent colleague, Terry Alderman, whilst Graeme Fowler reunited with 'Henry' Lawson. Allan Border declared that he was sick and tired of playing against the West Indies and who could blame him? When discussing Australia's England tour he sought an assurance that Garner would be rested when the Australians visit Taunton. Incidents from previous tours were relived and old jokes renewed as we slowly unwound together. Around midnight I walked back to the hotel for a slow bath, a hot hamburger and bed. It had been an exhausting day.

Next we moved up country to Ballarat and Bendigo for two more practice matches, the first against the Victorian state side, the second against their B team. On a bone hard, bouncy Ballarat wicket Tim

Robinson's right thumb was broken and Chris Cowdrey's forearm was badly bruised, injuries which would prevent them from being considered for selection for the rest of the tour. This reduced the squad to eleven fit men as Gatting had also damaged a hand in the game against Australia. I'm sure that these additional fixtures (England were the only side to play any friendlies) were great public relations exercises and they must have seemed like a jolly good idea ten months ago when the tour was planned but in fact they proved a liability. The rules of the competition did not allow any additions to the squad of fourteen; another injury at Bendigo and we might be taking the field against India with ten men. Moreover, after an arduous tour of India these matches became a chore for the English players whilst our opponents naturally warmed to the task of humiliating an international side. How we managed to escape with a victory at Ballarat, I'm still not sure. Dav Whatmore and Graham Yallop launched a fierce attack on our seamers, Edmonds and I retrieved the situation for a while, yet they needed only 15 runs from 6 overs with four wickets standing. Two brilliant catches by substitute fielder Richard Ellison plus more Australian panic gave us another four-run victory, which would have left Houdini himself dumbstruck. At Bendigo Downton scored a sparkling 111, Moxon an accomplished 95 and despite a lacklustre performance in the field we managed to win by the staggering margin of 23 runs. Things were going awry but no-one seemed capable of halting the slide.

Minor irritations began to assume far greater importance than they deserved. Allan Lamb innocently failed to attend a net practice because of a breakdown in communications; a cocktail party was sprung upon us with four hours' notice. Back in Sydney before our match against India, we arranged to practise in the nets just before dusk prior to fielding under lights; unfortunately this sensible idea was undermined by bad timing, the light permitting only four batsmen any worthwhile practice. Generally our preparation lacked the enthusiasm and self-discipline that had been a characteristic of the tour of India. Each of us should share the blame for that. Maybe international cricketers, simply because of their status, should have a greater sense of responsibility and should be capable of motivating themselves in every situation, but that has not been my experience; whether a player is representing Chewton Mendip 2nd XI or England he needs occasionally to be prodded in the right direction. In Australia it seemed that everyone from Gower downwards was too drained to provide that stimulus. The last three weeks of a tour can be a difficult, dangerous time. On my first tour in 1982/3 England went to New Zealand for three one-day internationals after four months in Australia and lost all three comfortably. Individually each one of us had every intention of trying our hardest, yet collectively there was no spark. Bob Willis, our captain, no matter how hard he tried, was incapable of arresting the decline; he was mentally exhausted, having devoted himself to the onerous task of tour captaincy for four months. I suspect that David Gower now experienced that same feeling of helplessness.

The Sydney Cricket Ground, the venue for our match against India, is now the most impressive cricketing arena in the world, in my opinion. The playing area is large enough not to strike fear into the hearts of slow off-spinners, yet the ground retains an intimacy that is not possible in such huge stadiums as Melbourne, Edgbaston or The Oval. The decrepit stands of two years ago have now been renovated with luxurious modern tip-up seats and it seemed to me that all that remains to be done is to fill up that green bit opposite the pavilion.

On a cloudy, humid afternoon Gower won the toss and asked India to bat and for fifteen overs Srikkanth exploited the wide open spaces. In this competition there are extra regulations about field placings; for fifteen overs just two boundary fielders are permitted and it is compulsory for two players to be in catching positions. Also, to my dismay, no more than five fielders can be placed on the leg side, thereby compelling an off-spinner to alter his normal one-day line and reducing his margin for error considerably. Srikkanth, with a stream of lofted drives on the off side, launched the Indian innings handsomely scoring 57 in just 53 balls. Unless you're bowling at him Srikkanth really is a delight to watch. Azharuddin failed, scoring a mere 45 and Kapil and Sunil, looking extremely relaxed now that he'd escaped from India, ensured a reasonable target for us to chase (235). On our part there was no lack of commitment in the field; Fowler hurled himself around the boundary, Cowans effected a run-out with a direct hit, Lamb was impeccable in the outfield, even Marks caught a catch at mid-wicket (Fowler, I'm please to report, was fielding at deep cover at the time). 235 was the sort of score that we kept attaining in India and with the score at 94–1 in the 24th over we seemed to be on target again. Yet by the 42nd over we have been dismissed for 149, the architect of India's victory was Sivaramakrishnan, later abetted by Ravi Shastri. Gower smacked a high full toss straight to deep mid-wicket, Lamb missed a googly and Moxon was caught and bowled. Siva, the god of destruction in the

Hindu pantheon, had struck again and as the required run rate increased we crumbled in a manner reminiscent of Ahmedabad to an inglorious, depressing defeat. Somehow the mischievous little man from Bombay had been able to rejuvenate the Indian side during the last three weeks. Yet such an overwhelming defeat reflected not only India's remarkable resurgence but also, with piercing clarity, our decline.

Worse was yet to come; at least the Athenians had had the option of packing their swords and sailing home, even if their pride rejected it. Against NSW B at Manly we were defeated by six wickets in another friendly. Those on the sidelines no doubt muttered about a lack of professionalism, the very quality that had been regarded as our saviour in India, yet I do not believe that this group of cricketers could ever be justly described as irresponsible.

We now needed some kind of mathematical miracle to enable us to qualify and 7,000 spectators ambled into the MCG to see whether we could perform one against Pakistan. A disciplined performance in the field restricted Pakistan to 213, with only Mudassar Nazar batting with any freedom. Returning to the cavernous Melbourne dressing rooms, David Gower was confronted with two choices, either to aim for a victory within 50 overs, which would not give us a chance of qualifying but would help to remove some of the egg from our faces or to attempt to score 214 in 32 overs. If this formidable target was achieved and India beat Australia then we might qualify. Gower, though aware of the possibility of us destructing like lemmings, opted for the latter. This was clearly the correct course to take even if it made our chances of victory more improbable. Whilst Allan Lamb was at the crease anything seemed possible as he produced a startling display of hitting; Imran Khan was thumped over the long-on boundary with staggering ease; the young left-arm seamer, Wasim Akram, who had earlier humbled the Australians with an astonishing five wicket opening spell, was consistently pulled and cut and not even his guru, Imran, at mid off, could provide him with the right answers. However when Allan was dismissed for 81 in just 69 balls as he miscued another projected drive, the innings inevitably lost its momentum. The middle order batsmen now collapsed in quick succession after a series of frenetic one-day dismissals – spooned catches and laughable run-outs – and we lost by 67 runs. For what it's worth I think that we would have won in normal circumstances, but Gower's decision to attempt victory in 32 overs was vindicated when India beat Australia the following day. The gamble, had it succeeded, would have ensured a place in the semi-finals.

So we solemnly packed our bags and organised travel arrangements. Several players decided to stay on in Australia for a while with their wives. Lamb, Edmonds and Fowler were shortly going to Calcutta to perform in a three-day jamboree there, whilst in three weeks time nine of the original sixteen would be heading for Sharjah under the captaincy of Norman Gifford for yet another one-day tournament. But for me the vitality of Sydney, the dust of Calcutta and the shekels of Sharjah could not match the attractions of the damp obscurity of Tiverton, though I knew that there would be the usual re-entry problems. My wife, like all cricketers' wives, had to become very independent. For a while I might seem an intruder in my own house, albeit a welcome one. Anna has had to adjust to being the head of a single-parent family for four and a half months and has no alternative but to create a rigid routine for survival and she will have ensured that it works. That routine will soon be shattered by my return and it will take a while to recreate a new and better one. For a week or two it will be impossible to find the car keys and the dog lead, the corkscrew and the cheque book and I'll be puzzled when my room service breakfast fails to appear at 8.15 prompt. I'm looking forward to it though.

I am now 30,000 feet above Muscat in a British Airways jumbo. Eight of the fourteen are here plus the management; Mike Gatting is still listening to Tina Turner, Richard Ellison is sipping champagne and Bernard Thomas is asleep in a position that only an Olympic gymnast could achieve. A smiling air hostess has just removed another plastic tray from in front of me – I've no idea whether it bore breakfast, lunch, tea or dinner – and it has occurred to me that our tour was like a succulent salmon sandwich made with stale bread; the bit in the middle was very good.

If we had returned after the Kanpur Test there would have been a heroes' welcome awaiting us at Heathrow, the sports columns would have been filled with glowing praise and unabashed optimism about the state of English cricket. Maybe the special nine-man committee, which has been set up by the TCCB to examine the organisation and the management of the English cricket team in view of 'recent dismal performances', would have been scrapped, but now I expect that Charles Palmer, who will chair this committee, will still be sending out his memos to his eight trusty cohorts. After Australia no-one quite knows what to think. Do our three defeats represent a minor relapse or the return of a long term cancerous growth? Well, that's for Charlie P and his boys to decide.

I do know that this summer's confrontation with Australia will be absolutely fascinating or as Pooh, the Swarup of the nursery, once said:

'Oh the honey bees are coming
On their little wings, and humming
That the summer, which is coming
Will be fun.'

Back in October I suggested, fairly seriously, that if Gower returned established as England's undisputed leader and if Gatting was firmly entrenched in England's middle order and with Botham rejuvenated, the Australians might be in for a bit of a shock. That has just about happened (only our performance in Australia introduces reservations). In India Gower, despite a disappointing series with the bat, steadily grew in stature in his own 'laid back', unobtrusive way; he was no less approachable than in the past and there were no clashes of personality and no threats to his authority. He was confident enough to trust his own judgements on the field and to manipulate his attack as he willed and he was fortunate to have a young, united side, who were always prepared to accept his decisions whether they seemed right or wrong. Before the tour began there was the odd question raised as to whether Phil Edmonds might unleash his independent streak to the detriment of everyone else, but we've seen how the Middlesex spinner toiled throughout the tour and how he became the lynchpin of the bowling in the Test matches. Gower clearly commanded Edmonds' respect and support even if there was the odd disagreement over technicalities and this was crucial to our success. The fascinating question this summer will be whether Gower can harness the awesome talent of Botham to the same effect. Ian, too, certainly respects David Gower and will support him, but will Gower have the strength to wrench the ball from Ian's hands in a Lord's Test match against Australia if he believes a change of bowling to be beneficial – or will he shrug his shoulders?

Botham himself will experience a new kind of pressure. Though there is still a gaping hole in the England side for him to fill, the Indian tour will have shown him that he's not indispensable; it is possible for England to win without him. I guess that he will have been slightly surprised by our success and particularly since this winter has not proved quite as peaceful as he would have hoped, he'll be anxious to make the headlines in June – for his cricketing prowess. Despite his prodigious Test record, he'll still have plenty to prove and that's when he's at his most dangerous as a cricketer.

There are of course others waiting to return, notably Gooch and Emburey. I imagine that both will be so grateful to be recalled to Test cricket that they would field at bat/pad and silly point for the entire series without complaint if Gower asked them to. No problems there for Gower, though the selectors may be scratching their heads when choosing England's most effective opening pair. Both Tim Robinson and Graeme Fowler, in their contrasting styles, had magnificent tours of India and if either is omitted from the First Test side, he can be considered unlucky. Whatever happens, both are sufficiently resilient and ambitious to ensure many more Tests for England. And, no doubt, Geoffrey will be expecting a recall as well. If England opt to play two spinners, which strikes me as a good idea if there is the slightest encouragement in the wickets, then I expect John Emburey to join with Edmonds to form arguably the best finger spinning combination in the world – whoops, there's always Derek Underwood as well. If the pitches in the summer of 1985 turn, I would back the English spinners to outbowl their Australian counterparts.

So far, on paper at least, this all looks very promising. If there is a weak link, it remains the pace attack. Neil Foster, after his staggering success in Madras, clearly deserves – and desperately wants – an extended run in the England team. He is still just 22 years of age and can only improve. At the moment his most likely partner would appear to be Norman Cowans even though he remains frustratingly inconsistent. There were times in India when he bowled with genuine hostility, embarrassing such accomplished players as Gavaskar and Vengsarkar, yet there were others, which usually coincided with the arrival of Amarnath at the wicket, when he was wayward and innocuous.

On the domestic scene every county cricketer will soon be studying his fixture list to check when he meets Middlesex, who could easily provide five of England's Test team. Apart from those already mentioned (Edmonds, Cowans and Emburey) Gatting and Downton will be certainties. Everyone knows that Gatting had a triumphant tour of India, but Paul Downton, true to form, remained something of an unsung hero; he averaged over 60 in the Test series, contributed vital runs in the one-day games and his wicketkeeping, if not flawless, gained in confidence as the tour progressed. He should remain a reassuring sight in one of the more peaceful corners of the English dressing room for years to come, phlegmatic, conscientious and quietly analysing how he can improve his game.

As for me, I'll remember my three and a half months in India, despite the international crises, the desperate poverty and the flat wickets, with far more pleasure than the month in Australia. It was a tremendous experience to tour with a successful side even if my own contributions were minor and sporadic. My publisher, I'm afraid, was right: 'A View from the Balcony' was a perfectly adequate title for all this. The long periods of being on the side-lines were frustrating, but I came to accept that situation, perhaps towards the end a little too readily for my own good. The lights of Melbourne, the razzmatazz of that opening ceremony and ignominy of Manly may soon fade from my memory but I'll not forget those feelings of bewilderment after the assassinations of Mrs Gandhi and Percy Norris, the euphoria after the Delhi Test, the visit to the Kali temple with Anna, the cricket match at the orphanage and the cheeful beggar in Chowringee Road.

England's tourists were easy to live with and when I'm old and grey (next September?) I'll be glad to recall the puerile pranks of Pocock and Fowler, the endless energy of Allan Lamb, Chris Cowdrey refusing to laugh at my best jokes just before Christmas, Richard Ellison, snoring, and Phil Edmonds always made me laugh even if he didn't mean to.

We're over Frankfurt now and I must bring this to a close. I quite like Eliot's 'Not with a bang, but a whimper' but it's been over-exposed lately. (I'm a little peeved that I used Chaucer's 'O moral Gower, this booke I direkte to thee' at the beginning, but anyway I was rather hoping that a few other people might buy it as well) and Horace's 'Exegi monumentum aere perennius' strikes me as a little pretentious for a tour book – I assume my readership needs no translation.

We're now leaving the coast of Europe heading for the Thames estuary. It is time to borrow Richard Ellison's aftershave.

ENGLAND v INDIA

Played at Sydney Cricket Ground
India won by 86 runs

INDIA

R. Shastri	c Fowler b Ellison	13
K. Srikkanth	run out	57
M. Azharuddin	c and b Cowans	45
D. Vengsarkar	run out	43
Kapil Dev	c Downton b Cowans	29
S. Gavaskar	not out	30
M. Amarnath	c Lamb b Cowans	6
R. Binny	c Marks b Foster	2
S. Madan Lal	c Downton b Foster	0
S. Viswanath	run out	8
Extras	(LB2)	2
Total	(9 wkts)	235

Fall of Wickets: 1–67, 2–74, 3–147, 4–183, 5–197, 6–216, 7–220, 8–220, 9–235.
Bowling: Cowans 10–0–59–3; Ellison 10–1–46–1; Foster 10–0–33–2; Edmonds 10–1–38–0; Marks 10–0–57–0.

ENGLAND

G. Fowler	c Viswanath b Binny	26
M. Moxon	c and b Sivaramakrishnan	48
D. Gower	c Vengsarkar b Sivaramakrishnan	25
A. Lamb	b Sivaramakrishnan	13
M. Gatting	c Viswanath b Shastri	7
P. Downton	c Shastri b Kapil Dev	9
V. Marks	st Viswanath b Shastri	2
P. Edmonds	st Viswanath b Shastri	5
R. Ellison	c Viswanath b Madan Lal	1
N. Foster	c Srikkanth b Madan Lal	1
N. Cowans	not out	3
Extras	(B3, LB4, W1, NB1)	9
Total		149

Fall of Wickets: 1–41, 2–94, 3–113, 4–126, 5–126, 6–130, 7–142, 8–144, 9–146, 10–149.
Bowling: Kapil Dev 7–0–21–1; Binny 8–0–33–1; Madan Lal 6.4–0–19–2; Sivaramakrishnan 10–0–39–3; Shastri 10–2–30–3.

AUSTRALIA v ENGLAND

Played at Melbourne Cricket Ground
Australia won by seven wickets

ENGLAND

G. Fowler	c and b McDermott	26
P. Downton	c McCurdy b McDermott	27
D. Gower	c Alderman b McCurdy	6
A. Lamb	c Kerr b Lawson	53
M. Gatting	c Alderman b O'Donnell	34
C. Cowdrey	lbw b McDermott	0
V. Marks	b Lawson	24
P. Edmonds	b Lawson	20
R. Ellison	not out	2
J. Agnew	not out	2
Extras	(B3, LB12, NB5)	20
Total	(8 wkts)	214

Fall of Wickets: 1–61, 2–66, 3–77, 4–159, 5–159, 6–166, 7–200, 8–211.
Bowling: Lawson 10–3–31–3; Alderman 10–0–48–0; McDermott 10–0–39–3; McCurdy 10–1–42–1; O'Donnell 9–0–39–1.

AUSTRALIA

K. Wessels	c Gatting b Ellison	39
R. Kerr	not out	87
K. Hughes	run out	0
A. Border	c Cowans b Marks	1
D. Jones	not out	78
Extras	(B1, NB6, LB3)	10
Total	(3 wkts)	215

Fall of Wickets: 1–57, 2–57, 3–58.
Bowling: Cowans 10–0–52–0; Ellison 10–4–34–1; Agnew 8–0–59–0; Marks 7.2–0–33–1; Edmonds 10–0–33–0.

ENGLAND v PAKISTAN

Played at Melbourne Cricket Ground
Pakistan won by 67 runs

PAKISTAN

Mudassar Nazar	c Foster b Edmonds	77
Moshin Khan	c Moxon b Ellison	9
Rameez Raja	c Moxon b Marks	21
Javed Miandad	c Downton b Foster	11
Imran Khan	b Ellison	35
Salim Malik	c Gatting b Foster	8
Qasim Omar	b Cowans	12
Tahir Naqqash	not out	21
Anil Dalpat	b Ellison	8
Azeem Hafeez	not out	0
Extras	(B5, LB4, W2)	11
Total	(8 wkts)	213

Fall of Wickets: 1–37, 2–93, 3–114, 4–126, 5–144, 6–181, 7–183, 8–212.
Bowling: Cowans 10–0–52–1; Ellison 10–0–42–3; Foster 10–0–56–2; Marks 10–2–25–1; Edmonds 10–1–29–1.

ENGLAND

G. Fowler	c Anil b Imran	0
D. Gower	c Tahir b Imran	27
A. Lamb	c Wasim b Azeem	81
M. Gatting	c Mudassar b Naqqash	11
P. Downton	run out	6
R. Ellison	c Anil b Tahir	6
V. Marks	run out	1
M. Moxon	c Imran b Azeem	3
P. Edmonds	not out	0
N. Foster	run out	1
N. Cowans	b Tahir	0
Extras	(B1, LB7, NB1, W1)	10
Total		146

Fall of Wickets: 1–0, 2–56, 3–102, 4–125, 5–138, 6–139, 7–141, 8–145, 9–146, 10–146.
Bowling: Imran Khan 7–0–33–2; Wasim Akram 10–0–59–0; Azeem Hafeez 3–0–22–2; Tahir Naqqash 4.2–0–24–3.

TEST MATCH AVERAGES

ENGLAND – BATTING AND FIELDING

	M	I	NO	Runs	HS	Average	100	50	Ct	St
M. W. Gatting	5	9	3	575	207	95.83	2	1	4	–
R. T. Robinson	5	9	2	444	160	63.42	1	2	–	–
P. R. Downton	5	6	3	183	74	61.00	–	2	14	2
G. Fowler	5	8	0	438	201	54.75	1	2	2	–
A. J. Lamb	5	7	1	241	67	40.16	–	3	9	–
P. H. Edmonds	5	6	0	175	49	29.16	–	–	–	–
D. I. Gower	5	7	1	167	78	27.83	–	1	6	–
C. S. Cowdrey	5	6	1	96	38	19.20	–	–	5	–
P. I. Pocock	5	5	2	39	22*	13.00	–	–	2	–
N. A. Foster	2	2	0	13	8	6.50	–	–	–	–
R. M. Ellison	3	4	0	12	10	3.00	–	–	–	–
N. G. Cowans	5	5	1	10	9	2.50	–	–	2	–

ENGLAND – BOWLING

	Overs	Mdns	Runs	Wkts	Average
N. A. Foster	87	18	286	14	20.42
P. H. Edmonds	276.1	104	584	14	41.71
N. G. Cowans	181.5	41	627	14	44.78
P. I. Pocock	237.5	53	655	13	50.38
C. S. Cowdrey	61	2	288	4	72.00
R. M. Ellison	105	24	289	4	72.25
M. W. Gatting	13	1	36	0	–

Also bowled: G. Fowler 1–1–0–0; D. I. Gower 3–0–13–0; A. J. Lamb 1–0–6–1; R. T. Robinson 1–1–0–0.

INDIA – BATTING AND FIELDING

	M	I	NO	Runs	HS	Average	100	50	Ct	St
M. Azharuddin	3	5	1	439	122	109.75	3	1	1	–
S. M. H. Kirmani	5	7	2	291	102	58.20	1	1	10	1
M. Amarnath	5	8	1	407	95	58.14	–	3	–	–
R. J. Shastri	5	9	2	383	142	54.71	2	1	4	–
K. Srikkanth	2	4	1	141	84	47.00	–	1	1	–
Kapil Dev	4	6	0	253	60	42.16	–	2	2	–
D. B. Vengsarkar	5	8	1	284	137	40.57	1	–	7	–
C. Sharma	3	4	3	40	17*	40.00	–	–	1	–
S. M. Patil	2	3	0	91	41	30.33	–	–	1	–
M. Prabhakar	2	4	1	86	35*	28.66	–	–	–	–
S. M. Gavaskar	5	8	0	140	65	17.50	–	1	3	–
L. Sivaramakrishnan	5	5	1	59	25	14.75	–	–	2	–
N. S. Yadav	4	6	3	43	28*	14.33	–	–	–	–
A. D. Gaekwad	3	5	0	71	28	14.20	–	–	2	–

Played in one Test: A. Malhotra 27; G. Sharma did not bat (10).

INDIA – BOWLING

	Overs	Mdns	Runs	Wkts	Average
M. Amarnath	21	4	49	2	24.50
L. Sivaramakrishnan	274.3	63	723	23	31.43
N. S. Yadav	34	31	362	9	40.22
Kapil Dev	161.5	33	436	10	43.60
G. Sharma	71	20	132	3	44.00
C. Sharma	50.3	6	200	4	50.00
R. J. Shastri	184	48	390	7	55.71
M. Prabhakar	29	4	102	1	102.00

Also bowled: M. Azharuddin 1–0–8–0; A. D. Gaekwad 1–0–1–0; S. M. Gavaskar 0.4–0–10–0; A. Malhotra 2–0–3–0; K. Srikkanth 2–0–11–0.

TOUR AVERAGES

BATTING AND FIELDING

	M	I	NO	Runs	HS	Average	100	50	Ct	St
M. W. Gatting	11	17	5	1029	207	85.75	3	4	10	–
M. D. Moxon	3	4	0	231	153	57.75	1	–	2	–
R. T. Robinson	11	18	3	861	160	57.40	3	3	1	–
G. Fowler	10	15	0	727	201	48.46	3	2	3	–
A. J. Lamb	10	14	2	441	67	36.75	–	4	13	–
D. I. Gower	11	15	1	482	86	34.42	–	4	10	–
N. A Foster	7	8	4	128	29	32.00	–	–	2	–
P. R. Downton	9	11	3	228	74	29.75	–	2	20	3
C. S. Cowdrey	9	11	1	211	70	21.10	–	1	9	–
V. J. Marks	6	8	1	142	66	20.28	–	1	1	–
P. H. Edmonds	11	12	0	241	49	20.08	–	–	5	–
R. M. Ellison	8	10	1	152	83*	16.88	–	1	2	–
P. J. W. Allott	3	3	1	29	14	14.50	–	–	–	–
B. N. French	4	5	0	63	19	12.60	–	–	12	2
P. I. Pocock	8	9	3	48	22*	8.00	–	–	2	–
N. G. Cowans	10	8	1	21	10	3.00	–	–	3	–

Played in one match: J. P. Agnew 12*.

BOWLING

	Overs	Mdns	Runs	Wkts	Average
N. A. Foster	230.1	58	655	29	22.58
J. P. Agnew	45	4	205	7	29.28
P. H. Edmonds	498.1	184	1019	32	31.84
N. G. Cowans	267.5	60	916	25	36.64
P. I. Pocock	321.1	73	932	23	40.52
V. J. Marks	121	28	321	7	45.85
C. S. Cowdrey	114	12	442	9	49.11
R. M. Ellison	210.1	57	550	11	50.00
M. W. Gatting	34	2	90	1	90.00
P. J. W. Allott	62.1	11	209	2	104.50

Also bowled: G. Fowler 1–1–0–0; D. I. Gower 3–0–13–0; A. J. Lamb 2–1–6–1; R. T. Robinson 1–1–0–0.